W9-BWL-623

Redeeming the Time

A Practical Guide to a Christian Man's Time Management

by Steven Maxwell

Communication
Concepts, Inc.

Redeeming the Time

Copyright © 2009 by Communication Concepts, Inc.

All rights reserved. Written permission must be secured from the publisher to use or reproduce any part of this book except for brief quotation in critical reviews or articles.

Ordering information:

Managers of Their Homes

1504 Santa Fe Street

Leavenworth, Kansas 66048

Phone: (913) 772-0392

Web: www.Titus2.com

Published by:

Communication Concepts, Inc.

Web: www.we-communicate.com

ACKNOWLEDGEMENTS

Scripture taken from the HOLY BIBLE, KING JAMES VERSION.

ISBN 978-0-9823003-0-5

Printed in the United States of America.

1   2

This book was created in Microsoft Word. QuarkXPress 6 and Adobe Photoshop were used for layout and design. All computers were Windows-based systems running Windows XP.

Cover design by Christopher and Joseph Maxwell. Inside design and layout by Sarah Maxwell.

The book is dedicated to:

My faithful wife and teammate, Teri. She has been such an amazing help throughout this book project, and I'm so grateful to the Lord Jesus for her.

Table of Contents

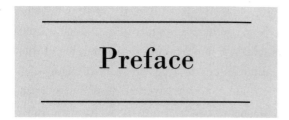

Preface

For many years I have wanted to write a book to challenge and help Christian men be the fathers and husbands that the Lord Jesus Christ would have them be. When the Lord put on my heart that it was time to write such a resource, I next had to seek Him for the theme of the book. He led me to time management as being the key to every aspect of our lives.

There are many time-management books available. However, most don't address time management from a biblical perspective. "All scripture *is* given by inspiration of God, and *is* profitable for doctrine, for reproof, for correction, for instruction in righteousness" (2 Timothy 3:16). We usually look for "five easy steps to. . . ." That is not what you will find here. Instead, I have taken Scripture and my personal experience with time pressure to put together information that I believe will help you manage your time.

I am grateful for the assistance my precious wife provides for my writing by brainstorming with me, and then editing and revising by my side. The Lord has made us a team, and I rely on her help.

My two oldest sons, Nathan and Christopher, ages 32 and 30, read the manuscript in order to give me feedback. Christopher and Joseph designed the cover, and Sarah (27) proofreads and imports the text into the layout software. Anna (16) and Mary (13) took over many of my wife's daily tasks through the summer so she could help me with this project.

I invited twelve men who were interested in time management to read the book, write comments on it, fill out a questionnaire, make a schedule, and begin using it. I felt ten of their schedules, plus Nathan and mine, might be helpful examples to be included in the book. The men worked under tight deadlines, giving us valuable feedback. I am thankful for their input. We also have a professional proofreader, and we have benefitted from her expertise on this project.

I pray the Lord Jesus will use this material in a very practical way to teach you to redeem your time and give you a realistic time-management plan.

Steve Maxwell

Can He Manage His Time?

"I am blessed to have a family-loving, hard-working husband. He strives to follow Jesus in all he does. His lack of time for areas he sees as critical is a constant source of frustration for him. He wants to be 'in the fight' to reclaim our country for Christ, but he struggles with having enough energy left over after work to even do family devotions (although he still leads our family in devotions several times a week). He is constantly tired and drained. We are praying the Lord will give us a solution to this frustrating problem of not having enough time and energy to do the things he wants to do and feels the Lord is leading him to do. He must not be the only man that feels this way, but so far we have no solutions."

This wife's comments concerning her husband and his time pressure are quite typical. In this crazy, fast-paced society in which we live, most men feel tremendous pressure to accomplish all that needs to be done with little hope of time left for what they would like to do. They have their jobs that, with a commute, may take them away from home for ten or more hours a day. If they are self-employed, the pressure can be as bad, if not worse, in feeling the need to make one more call or quote before ending the day. Then, there is a house that requires maintenance and yard upkeep. There may be several vehicles to service. In fact, the more we own, the more time is required for Dad to keep it all running.

To add to those time pressures, family members have expectations of Dad and what he should be accomplishing. Mom wants him to bring home a paycheck that keeps pace with rising costs, spend time with her, help with the children, and remodel the house. The children demand Dad's attention in a host of varying situations and at different, but quite immediate, moments in time. Dad's boss says he is to put in more hours and turn out more work. The church asks for Dad's time in tasks that range from attendance at services to ministry efforts and men's groups. Last, but certainly not least, the Lord wants a man's heart, soul, and mind, which will definitely impact his time.

It all comes back to a constant drain on the well of hours from which Dad goes to draw. Even in our modern world of instant everything, no one has found a way to reproduce or provide more time for Dad to accomplish what he should do. With these kinds of daily pressures, when Dad comes home from work each evening, he often brings his frustration with him.

"My husband is very tired most of the time. There are many nights when he only gets five hours of sleep. He is self-employed in two different businesses. The house and yard are a mess. Thankfully the cars are fairly new and don't need much looking after. On days when he is home, he doesn't stop moving except to sit at the computer. Our life is crazy and completely unorganized."

An Abundant Life?

There was a time when I was struggling greatly to be the "perfect" employee, husband, father, church member, and Christian. I found it frustrating and finally realized it was impossible with the twenty-four hours I had available. Have you had a similar experience?

In John 10:10 we read what Jesus said: "… I am come that they might have life, and that they might have *it* more abundantly." Where is this abundant life when one is living with continual time pressure? The Greek word for "abundantly" is *perissos,* and according to *Strong's Talking Greek and Hebrew Dictionary* it means "exceedingly, beyond measure." This is the life that the Lord Jesus has promised to us.

Obviously the abundant life doesn't mean a life void of problems since we read a few chapters later, in John 16:33, about tribulation: "These things I have spoken unto you, that in me ye might have peace. In the world ye shall have tribulation: but be of good cheer; I have overcome the world." Here the Greek word for "tribulation" means "affliction, anguish, burdened, and trouble." Many will quickly agree that sounds much more like their life.

So on the one hand, we read that Jesus has given us a super-abundant life. It is beyond measure. On the other hand, He has promised us tribulation. One might think that an abundant life would not involve tribulation. How can the two be harmonized?

I hope to show you in this book that when we are following our Lord Jesus, we can have peace from time pressures. We have the same twenty-four hours that every other human being has, and yet the Lord will pack more value into that time than we can on our own. When we yield our days to Him, He will accomplish more than we ever would dream of accomplishing. As you look back over the years, you will say, "Ah, Lord God. Truly, I stand amazed at what You have done with so little! All praise be to You, Father." That is the wonder of a yielded life. He takes our ashes—time pressure—and turns it into beauty—peace and productivity. He takes our pitiful pot of time and makes it the widow's oil.

Numbering and Redeeming

"So teach *us* to number our days, that we may apply *our* hearts unto wisdom" (Psalms 90:12). The Lord wants us to learn to value our time. This education will be a process that requires obedience to the Lord Jesus Christ. As we learn to number our days, it will help us to make wise choices in how we utilize that time.

The following two verses show us that the Lord Jesus Christ is interested in how we use our time: "Walk in wisdom toward them that are without, redeeming the time" (Colossians 4:5). "Redeeming the time, because the days are evil" (Ephesians 5:16). The Greek word used here for redeem is *exagorazo*. As it is used in these verses, it means:

> "to buy up, to buy up for one's self, for one's use, to make wise and sacred use of every opportunity for doing good, so that zeal and well doing are as it were the purchase money by which we make the time our own."

In essence, these verses are saying that we are to purchase back our time by how we are investing and managing that time.

Comments

In this book, you will find three kinds of comments. First, we are using feedback from a survey we took of a large number of conservative Christian families to evaluate the issues men were facing with their time usage. We planned to use the information to help us with the direction of this book and to give us statistics. We received much more than that through the comments that were included by the survey participants in an area for personal feedback. The survey could be filled out by a husband, or wife. We received many heart cries from wives concerned about their husband's time and how they were spending it. We share those throughout the book as examples of the problems that are being encountered by men with their time.

Secondly, you will discover "sticky notes" that contain comments from the men who read the manuscript of this book and gave us feedback concerning it. Many of their comments we collected and inserted for your benefit. Thirdly, we have used e-mails and experiences from our personal lives. We have received permission to use all of the comments that you find in this book.

What Is Required

I sometimes think how easy it would be if the Lord just did it all for us. In the blink of an eye, we would have no more time pressures because everything that needed attention, He would have already taken care of. But the Lord doesn't work that way, even though we know He most certainly could.

The Lord could have built a boat for Noah prior to the flood as opposed to it taking Noah up to a hundred years to build it. When He sent the children of Israel into Canaan, He could have wiped out the nations ahead of them. He didn't. When Jesus raised Lazarus from the dead, He first asked some men to remove the stone, but He could have spoken a word and had it go flying off into the air. The Lord doesn't need our efforts. Nonetheless, He requires them. As James 2:26 says, ". . . faith without works is dead. . . ."

We have to accept the fact that any solution to managing our time will take effort and attention on our part. It won't happen automatically or because we wish it would.

Be determined not only to taste of the abundant life Jesus has promised us, but also to feed on it. This book will help you because it is not built on anyone's creativity, but rather upon the Word of God. When we are willing to base our life on the truth of Scripture, we are building upon the solid rock. "Whosoever cometh to me, and heareth my sayings, and doeth them, I will shew you to whom he is like: He is like a man which built an house, and digged deep, and laid the foundation on a rock: and when the flood arose, the stream beat vehemently upon that house, and could not shake it: for it was founded upon a rock" (Luke 6:47-48). It is not enough to know truth, but we must obey truth. "But be ye doers of the word, and not hearers only, deceiving your own selves" (James 1:22). Are you willing to begin an exciting journey today? It will cost you effort, but what do you have to lose except for frustration, guilt, and worry?

We will stand before the King of kings one day and give an account for the responsibilities He has entrusted us with. He will judge whether we used our time wisely or squandered that time on things of little value. It should put a healthy sense of terror in our hearts knowing we will have all the details of our lives examined before His throne. There are things in my life that I now regret having wasted precious time on.

The concepts in this book have been useful to me in separating the gold, silver, and precious stones that have lasting value from the wood, hay, and straw that will be burnt up. Read this book, and prayerfully consider what Mr. Maxwell has to say about biblical responsibilities. Your life will be blessed by it.

CHAPTER

2

Whose Time Is It?

The basis for time management will be a determination of who owns my time. If it is my time, then I choose how to spend that time based upon my preferences, wants, and desires. Certainly this is a prevalent philosophy in our world today, and it goes something like this: "I work because I have to work since I like to eat, and I like what my money buys me. When work is over, though, I will spend my time in whatever manner most pleases me. After all, I have worked hard, and I deserve it."

However, if I am responsible for using my time in different ways, or if the time isn't really my time, that will have a great impact on my time management. I will make decisions for how my time is used based on a completely different set of priorities.

The "Mine" Mentality

I think most dads can remember a time of watching two or more children play and observing what happens when one of the children takes a toy from the other. Usually the response from the now-toyless child is a loud exclamation—"MINE!"— accompanied by a quick attempt to retrieve the stolen toy. Depending on the children's ages, things may now escalate into a toddler brawl of sorts. Isn't it amazing at what a young age we learn to be possessive of our "things"?

I remember when I purchased my first car. I was fifteen, and it was a 1957 Chevy sedan with a six-cylinder automatic transmission. I bought it from my mom because the transmission was going out, and it would have been expensive for her to repair. With a crescent wrench, I began to take out the motor and transmission to be replaced with a small V8 and four speed that I had found inexpensively. I spent many hours on that car, and after it was painted, I sure was proud of it. There was no doubt about it. It was MY car, and I could do what I wanted to do with it. In the same way, there have been a host of things through the years that I have owned, and my mindset has usually been the same. "MINE!"

Let me share with you a story from Scripture. "And the children of Israel did evil again in the sight of the LORD, and served Baalim, and Ashtaroth, and the gods of Syria, and the gods of Zidon, and the gods of Moab, and the gods of the children of Ammon, and the gods of the Philistines, and forsook the LORD, and served not him. And the anger of the LORD was hot against Israel, and he sold them into the hands of the Philistines, and into the hands of the children of Ammon" (Judges 10:6-7). Those Israelites were doing what they pleased. They were saying of their lives—"Mine!"

> I used to fish on weekends sometimes with family and sometimes not. I gave back the boat to Dad, and now do projects with my family every weekend. My son has said how great it is with no TV because now we do projects together.

I think this is often the way we find ourselves living as well. I am doing what I choose to do with my life because it is mine! Here's an example of this that was shared with us:

"My husband is introverted and needs time to himself to maintain emotional health. That is much of the reason for

his time on the computer. However, I can't help but notice sometimes that he doesn't put in near the number of work hours that I do!"

When we believe that our lives are our possessions to direct as we prefer, it is easy to make choices for how we live our lives and how we use our time based on what we want to do. We can feel like this man who has decided he needs time to himself for his emotional health, and then decides that he will retreat to the computer for that time.

God's Ownership

God's perspective on ownership, however, is vastly different from the thoughts of mankind. He says, "For every beast of the forest *is* mine, *and* the cattle upon a thousand hills" (Psalms 50:10). This verse tells us that He owns it all. That is a pretty clear statement concerning what I might think are my personal possessions, but what about my life itself? Scripture tells us that those who have made a profession of faith in Jesus Christ for salvation belong to Him! "For ye are bought with a price: therefore glorify God in your body, and in your spirit, which are God's" (1 Corinthians 6:20). Just in case one verse wasn't enough, let's also look to another: "Ye are bought with a price; be not ye the servants of men" (1 Corinthians 7:23). We are owned by Jesus. His ownership of us was acquired through a purchase transaction.

> He owns us, and we can trust He will guide what He owns.

An important question for each man to ask himself is: "Am I owned by the Lord Jesus?" Paul exhorted us: "Examine yourselves, whether ye be in the faith; prove your own selves. Know ye not your own selves, how that Jesus Christ is in you, except ye be reprobates?" (2 Corinthians 13:5). Are we in the faith? Is Jesus our Savior? Prove yourself, and don't be easy about it. Where you will spend eternity is too important to be unsure.

I've know many dads who go to church but seem to have no real relationship with Jesus. Fundamentally, salvation has little to do with being a member of a church, but it has everything to do with whether each is a child of the Living God. I will list a few Scriptures below that highlight how a person becomes a Christian.

- "For all have sinned, and come short of the glory of God" (Romans 3:23). Each of us has broken God's law and is a sinner before God.

- "But the fearful, and unbelieving, and the abominable, and murderers, and whoremongers, and sorcerers, and idolaters, and all liars, shall have their part in the lake which burneth with fire and brimstone: which is the second death" (Revelation 21:8). As sinners we are condemned to hell.

- "And the times of this ignorance God winked at; but now commandeth all men every where to repent" (Acts 17:30). We must repent of our sin.

- "Marvel not that I said unto thee, Ye must be born again" (John 3:7). We must be born again.

- "For by grace are ye saved through faith; and that not of yourselves: *it is* the gift of God: Not of works, lest any man should boast" (Ephesians 2:8-9). Pray and ask Jesus to save you and come into your life. Each must place his faith in Jesus, Who died on the cross to pay for our sins.

- "That if thou shalt confess with thy mouth the Lord Jesus, and shalt believe in thine heart that God hath raised him from the dead, thou shalt be saved. For with the heart man believeth unto righteousness; and with the mouth confession is made unto salvation.

For the scripture saith, Whosoever believeth on him shall not be ashamed. . . . For whosoever shall call upon the name of the Lord shall be saved" (Romans 10:9-11,13). Tell others that you have placed your faith in Jesus, and He is now your Savior.

- "As newborn babes, desire the sincere milk of the word, that ye may grow thereby" (1 Peter 2:2). As a newborn babe, in Christ, commit to reading His Word every day that you may grow thereby. We will address this point at length in this book.

The Apostle John tells us that we can know that we are saved. "These things have I written unto you that believe on the name of the Son of God; that ye may know that ye have eternal life, and that ye may believe on the name of the Son of God" (1 John 5:13). I encourage you to settle this question right now if you have any doubts. The rest of this book builds upon the premise of salvation.

If we are owned by Jesus, what really does He own? He owns it all: our vehicles, our property, our houses, our other possessions, our money, our bodies, our abilities, and our TIME! The primary emphasis of this book is "our" time, and now we learn that it isn't really our time at all, but His time that we are discussing. What an amazing realization. It isn't "mine" like I have always thought it was, but instead, it is His time.

My Awareness

The ramifications of being owned by Christ can be troubling to me. Before my salvation on December 7th of 1975, I was accustomed to thinking "mine" in regards to my life. Since then, I have been coming to a gradual understanding of what it means to be owned by Jesus Christ, and I think there is still much more the Lord will be teaching me in this area of His ownership. The struggle in this process is letting go of aspects of my life that I have held onto strongly for so many years and truly yielding them to Him.

Did you know that the abundant life that Jesus promises to believers comes when one is yielded to His ownership? It is found in the man who is at peace knowing he is wholly Jesus' possession and obeying Him. Jesus used the example of sheep following the voice of their shepherd in giving us the picture of one having the abundant life. "But he that entereth in by the door is the shepherd of the sheep. To him the porter openeth; and the sheep hear his voice: and he calleth his own sheep by name, and leadeth them out. And when he putteth forth his own sheep, he goeth before them, and the sheep follow him: for they know his voice. . . . The thief cometh not, but for to steal, and to kill, and to destroy: I am come that they might have life, and that they might have *it* more abundantly" (John 10:2-4, 10).

The sheep that obeys the shepherd has protection and peace as it follows. However, the sheep that disobeys and strays can expect hardship and the shepherd's rod. We like the benefits of being saved from an eternity in hell and being with Jesus forever, but the idea of ownership can be a tough pill to swallow. We won't begin to properly manage our time from God's perspective, though, until we have a grasp on whose time it really is and the necessity of surrendering to the Shepherd.

If we understand that we are owned by the Lord Jesus and that our time is truly His time, we see that time is precious, far above gold. We want to please Him, Who gave His life to redeem us to Himself. "Forasmuch as ye know that ye were not redeemed with corruptible things, *as* silver and gold, from your vain conversation *received* by tradition from your fathers; But with the precious blood of Christ, as of a lamb without blemish and without spot" (1 Peter 1:18-19). Our desire should be to please Jesus even more than ourselves or others with how we spend our time.

The Perspective

Another aspect of God owning our time has to do with how much time we have. There is the realization that when the time "well" is empty, this life on earth is over. My family attends church in a nursing home, and the brothers and sisters of our fellowship are "biding their time" as they wait to pass into eternity. We are regularly called to the deathbeds of those who are in our church. Watching others whose time is finished has allowed me to have a new perspective on the value of the time the Lord Jesus has assigned to me. If only everyone could come to the point of realizing that when the appointed time has come, there is nothing that can be done to prolong life. This emphasizes the importance of how valuable our time really is.

When each second is gone, it is gone forever. At that point, we can not redeem it. I tell the children that our time is like a giant jar filled with pennies that we are just barely able to carry about. Each penny represents a minute of life. However, there is a small hole in the bottom of the jar from which pennies fall out to the floor. *Tink, tink, tink,* go the pennies as they hit the ground. There is no way to put any pennies back into the jar, and when the last one drops out, they are gone. When we breathe that final breath, our life on earth is over. There is simply nothing more precious than our time because we can't do anything to replenish it. "Whereas ye know not what *shall be* on the morrow. For what *is* your life? It is even a vapour, that appeareth for a little time, and then vanisheth away" (James 4:14). What will we do with the time that we have that is slowly slipping away? Will we redeem it?

Wasting Time

"My husband loves to sit in front of an electronic box and becomes offended when asked to do otherwise. The children have verbalized that they don't get enough time with Dad."

Isn't this what can happen when we view our time as belonging to us? We choose what to do with that time based on our desires and preferences. However, as we learn to see that our time is really His time, it becomes imperative that we don't waste time. Any time wasted is time that can't be redeemed and less that will be achieved.

Years ago I saw a video of an assembly line. Each person put a specific part on the product that was being built. They had to do their job in the limited amount of time they had while the product was in front of them. If they were too slow about it, or diverted their attention to something else, they would miss the opportunity, and the product would be rejected because it was incomplete.

If we aren't diligent with the time we have, there can be eternal consequences for which we are responsible. "For unto every one that hath shall be given, and he shall have abundance: but from him that hath not shall be taken away even that which he hath. And cast ye the unprofitable servant into outer darkness: there shall be weeping and gnashing of teeth" (Matthew 25:29-30).

The worldly Christian says of his time, "I want to spend my time in the most pleasurable way I can!" He is anxious to get through with or avoid what he should do so that he can get to what he considers to be fun. The believer pleads, "Lord Jesus, my time is slipping away. Please help me to spend every minute as You would have me to spend it." What is our attitude about our time? Unless we see it as the most valuable thing we have next to Jesus Himself, we will be prone to squandering it like the prodigal son.

Have you ever noticed that when you borrow an item, you tend to be even more careful with it than you might have been if it had been your own? I think this concept comes into play when we grab hold of the fact that our time is His time. It puts a new perspective on our responsibility toward time usage, how we are to manage it, and the desire not to waste it.

Are There Consequences?

Let's go back to the story from Judges where the Israelites were living their lives as if they owned them and ignoring the fact that they were owned by Another. From our perspective, we would all agree that this was a serious misjudgment on their part because we can read the outcome of their decisions. They were, in fact, not able to do as they pleased in choosing how they spent their days because God owned them, and they had previously been given direction such as the one found in Exodus 20:3: "Thou shalt have no other gods before me."

It wasn't a brief period of consequences that they received because of the men's wrong choices—it was eighteen years! "And that year they vexed and oppressed the children of Israel: eighteen years, all the children of Israel that *were* on the other side Jordan in the land of the Amorites, which *is* in Gilead" (Judges 10:8). As a result of their disobedience, their families suffered too. It really didn't matter whether those Israelites agreed with the consequences, whether they thought their actions deserved eighteen years of hardship, or whether they believed God owned them. The only opinion that mattered was that of the God of Creation's. His ownership was proved by His ability to chasten them for their disobedience. Obviously, He decided eighteen years was the perfect consequence for their sin. God did what He chose to do with His people because He owned them. "For whom the Lord loveth he chasteneth, and scourgeth every son whom he receiveth" (Hebrews 12:6). We can expect chastening if we don't obey the Father as He directs us in how to use our time.

Worth noting is that God is not a mean, vengeful God who delights in punishing His children. God's consequence was for the good of His people. He had given them clear commands, but they disobeyed. It is much like the dad who has taught his child how to play with other children. When his child takes a toy from another, the father gives the child a consequence. The father knows his child needs to learn proper behavior or there will be far worse consequences in his life for stealing.

Freedom from Time's Stress

If we don't start to view our time as being precious and owned by our Savior, the One Who bought us, we will certainly make mistakes with our time usage—perhaps grave mistakes with grave consequences. The Lord has deemed that we each have only twenty-four hours in a day, and that is all we have with which to work. At some point, many men come to realize that they have a time crisis. They are simply out of time, and no matter what they do, it doesn't seem to get any better. Could it be that these time pressures and the stress they cause us to feel are the beginning of consequences from the Lord when He is trying to get our attention?

There are so many demands on our time. These demands can put much pressure on us, both directly by words and indirectly, by insinuations and attitudes. If we truly are owned by the Lord Jesus, then He is the One we must be committed to pleasing. God's ownership of us and our time frees us from the stress we often carry in regard to our time. If we are obedient to His direction, He owns responsibility for what gets done and what doesn't. Since it is His time, He manages the time, and He will do a much better job of managing it than we will do. "Come unto me, all *ye* that labour and are heavy laden, and I will give you rest. Take my yoke upon you, and learn of me; for I am meek and lowly in heart: and ye shall find rest unto your souls. For my yoke *is* easy, and my burden is light" (Matthew 11:28-30). We have to be listening to Him and receiving our direction from Him. He will not give us more to do than we can accomplish in our lives because He has given us exactly the amount of time we need to complete what He has called us to do.

My Time Is His Time

God owns it all. We have grown up with the "mine" mindset. We can live our lives thinking we own our time, and we can do what we want to do with it. That doesn't change the reality that it is really God's time. If we will submit to God's ownership of our time, we will view our time in a totally different perspective than if we claim its ownership.

What makes our time even more precious is that we are bought with a price, the blood of the Lord Jesus. "Much more then, being now justified by his blood, we shall be saved from wrath through him" (Romans 5:9). We can choose to value that time, knowing we only have so much of it, or we can waste it away minute by minute. As we obey the Lord's leading for our time, we will leave behind the stress that many are living with when they face time pressures beyond their time resources. We step into the abundant life Jesus has promised to believers.

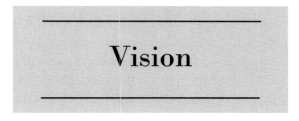

Vision

"My husband is a good man, but he has no goals nor does he want them. He plays on the computer from the time he is home till he decides to go to bed."

Having no goals would be fairly typical even among Christian families. If we want to be good managers of our time, it begins by understanding what is important in our lives so we know where to spend our time. Otherwise we can feel like we are on a frantic time treadmill, racing for all we are worth with no relief in sight. Rather than being able to focus our attention on the real needs for our time usage, we find ourselves doing what we have always done, with new tasks regularly added in but nothing taken out.

Because knowing where we are going is so important to time management, I want to help you see what happens when we don't have goals for our own lives and our family's lives or if those goals are too general. In addition, we will evaluate how these goals affect our time.

I like to use the word *vision* when referring to personal and family goals. To me the word *vision* communicates the importance of involving the Lord in the long-range direction of my time. "Where *there is* no vision, the people perish. . ." (Proverbs 29:18).

As a youth I used to enjoy going squirrel hunting on my uncle's farm in southern Iowa. With my .22 rifle in hand, I would walk slowly through the woods attempting not to make noise as I stepped on crunchy leaves. Hunting a small animal with a .22 is not as easy as it would be with a shotgun. I first had to get close to the squirrel, and then it took a steady, careful shot to bring one home. I wasn't overly successful because the dry leaves were loud, I wasn't that great a shot, and I had little heart for the killing aspect. I mostly loved just being out in the woods. The point of my hunting story is that if you don't aim at something carefully, you aren't going to hit it. The inverse is also true: if you aim at nothing, you will hit nothing.

Do You Have a Vision?

"As far as a vision statement, I have one for my children and their education. As a family, we don't have one, unfortunately. I have been praying that my husband would become interested in our homeschooling and one day care about creating a vision statement for our family. That is my desire, and I am trusting the Lord will help us with that. My husband dislikes attending church, to say the least; however, he has a website in hopes of reaching non-believers and cult members. He spends a lot of time on the Internet and doing outreach to cult members. Unfortunately and sadly, I don't think he has things in order or priorities right at home. For a while he was trying to change things around, but I am afraid other things are more important to him right now."

We often ask, "Would God say this is the best way to spend our time?"

Without a vision, we can be easily sidetracked—perhaps even to good activities, but missing what are the most important uses of our time. Don't sacrifice what is best for what is good. The man in this example is spending his time in ways he believes will build God's kingdom, but in the process of that, he is neglecting his vital priority, which is his family.

One dad wrote me an e-mail, and he told how his children are all headed for hell. He felt that he had "showed them the way." He described himself as a typical "token Christian," but Jesus wasn't his Lord. He spent his time doing what he felt like doing without any concern for following the Lord Jesus. He had no goals for his life but lived to make money, have fun, and not be bothered by his children. He was content to go to work and then spend his evenings watching TV. His children are following in his footsteps.

"And, ye fathers, provoke not your children to wrath: but bring them up in the nurture and admonition of the Lord" (Ephesians 6:4). This man didn't involve himself in his children's lives spiritually when they were growing up, but rather he let his wife be the spiritual teacher. All she ever wanted was children who loved the Lord Jesus. Sadly, the children have followed his example rather than his wife's. He managed his time in the way he wanted to manage it. He now acknowledges responsibility for leading his children on the path toward hell. He feels unable to direct them spiritually because of his own spiritual bankruptcy. Even if he knew how to help his children, they want nothing to do with him. They hate him because he lived his life selfishly and had no time for them. What heavy guilt to live with for the rest of his life! Here we can see that the repercussions of having no goals go way beyond living without time-management guidelines.

Where Are You Aiming?

I remember many years ago when I was graduating from high school, people would ask me, "What are you going to do after you graduate?" Some things never change. Our children are asked that same question.

What if you were to ask a youth at your church about his future after graduation, and his answer was simply, "I want to have fun and be happy." After thinking about that response, you might draw a number of conclusions such as:

He has no real idea what he wants to accomplish.

He has no ambition or drive.

He has such a low expectation, he probably won't achieve even the goal of being happy.

Now ask yourself what you are aiming for in your life and with your family? Are your goals any higher than the high school graduate who wants to be happy?

During our travels, we have spoken with many families around this continent. From discussions with them, it is evident that the vast majority of families have very little, if any, direction for their lives. Consequently, they have no barometer for how to use their time.

The Bible Has the Answers

If we are going to have goals, doesn't it make sense that they would be good ones? This book is written for Christians, those bought with the blood of the Lord Jesus. We are not our own. Therefore, it shouldn't be a matter of the goals we want, but what the Lord Jesus wants for us. The servant doesn't choose how he will spend his time, but the Master specifies what he is to do. How does someone determine what the Lord wants for his life and for each family member? What would this vision entail and how would one use it in helping him manage his time?

The Lord has told us plainly what He desires for our lives. "All scripture *is* given by inspiration of God, and *is* profitable for doctrine, for reproof, for correction, for instruction in righteousness: That the man of God may be perfect, throughly furnished unto all good works" (2 Timothy 3:16-17). The Lord has given us the Bible by which to live. It is the master vision for our lives. However, there is so much information in the Bible that it can be difficult to set specific, definable goals. Therefore, it is beneficial if we narrow our vision down to several statements that reflect the direction God is calling us personally and as a family.

We begin by praying and seeking succinct direction from the Word. I have found that the amount of time I pray is an inverse indicator of my pride. If I don't spend my time praying, asking the Lord to show me how to best utilize my time and lead my family, it means that I don't really believe prayer is important, and I am making the decisions on my own. Jesus said in Matthew 26:41, "Watch and pray, that ye enter not into temptation: the spirit indeed *is* willing, but the flesh *is* weak."

You will find that as you read the Bible each day, the Lord puts certain verses on your heart for your personal life and for your family. If you write them down, over time you will develop a road map for where the Lord wants to take your family. By basing your vision on Scripture, you don't have to be concerned about getting off track with it. The Lord will always lead you consistently with Scripture.

Let's Get Practical

I recall many times on the way home after church when my wife, Teri, would say, "What a great message, but I want to know how to apply it to my life." No matter how good something sounds, if it can't be applied, then where is the benefit? "All things are lawful for me, but all things are not expedient: all things are lawful for me, but all things edify not" (1 Corinthians 10:23).

Our vision statement provides direction for our time management. For the sake of example, let's now evaluate my family's current vision statement and see how it directs my use of time. I say "current" because I always have the freedom to add to it as the Lord leads.

As you read through my vision statement, notice how every item has a Scripture reference associated with it. No matter how good a goal might be, if it doesn't originate in God's Word, I don't want it as a goal. Remember we are owned by the Lord Jesus.

Maxwell Family Vision Statement

By God's grace, each member of the family would have a saving knowledge of the Lord Jesus Christ and serve Him (John 3:16, Hebrews 9:14) and:

- joyfully serve others (Galatians 5:13, Colossians 3:17, Romans 12:1)

- be obedient (John 14:15)

- respect others (Romans 12:10)

- be self-disciplined (Galatians 5:23)

- love children (Matthew 19:14)

- pursue holiness (Romans 12:1, Titus 1:8, 1 Peter 1:15-16)

- court and not date (Romans 12:1)

- live as ambassadors for Christ, including speaking, writing, and dressing appropriately (Colossians 3:17)

- be lovers of God more than lovers of pleasures (2 Timothy 3:4)

- learn to edify rather than criticize (Romans 14:19, 1 Thessalonians 5:11)

- be content (Philippians 4:11)

- be "wise unto that which is good, and simple concerning evil" (Romans 16:19)

- love His Word, have a good understanding of the Bible and church doctrine (2 Timothy 2:15)

- give their hearts to us as long as they are living in our home (Proverbs 23:26)

- be debt free even for cars and houses (Proverbs 22:7, Romans 13:8)

Vision Directs Time Usage

The overriding point on my vision statement is that each one in my family has a saving knowledge of Jesus and a real relationship with Him. That is where it all begins, and little matters if the child has no relationship with Jesus. "For what is a man profited, if he shall gain the whole world, and lose his own soul? or what shall a man give in exchange for his soul?" (Matthew 16:26). I look at our family time in the Word as being the number-one contributor to leading my children to salvation. That investment of time is directed and substantiated by my vision statement.

The first subpoint of my vision statement is that my children would joyfully serve others. As I have spoken with many men who profess faith in Jesus but acknowledge no power or vibrancy in their relationship with Him, it becomes obvious that they haven't obeyed the Lord Jesus by serving others. "Yea, a man may say, Thou hast faith, and I have works: shew me thy faith without thy works, and I will shew thee my faith by my works" (James 2:18). Faith and works go hand in hand. Salvation comes through faith, and works will follow if it is real salvation. Many men go off by themselves to minister to others.

Sadly, they miss out on a bonus for their time had they included their families and given them the appetite, blessing, and reality of Jesus in their lives by serving together.

I invest time ministering with my family because that leads my children to learn to joyfully serve others. An example of serving the Lord alongside my children is that for over ten years our family held a small church service at a local nursing home every other Saturday afternoon. Also for over ten years, we went to a homeless shelter and led a chapel service the second Saturday of every month. We have had some wonderful experiences in serving Jesus this way, and I have seen firsthand the way that this use of my time has developed in my children joyful hearts of service.

Following salvation, a very critical aspect of life in Christ is obeying Him. "He that hath my commandments, and keepeth them, he it is that loveth me: and he that loveth me shall be loved of my Father, and I will love him, and will manifest myself to him" (John 14:21). I want my children to be aware of Jesus Christ living in them and others to observe Jesus in my children as well. In John 14:21 we are told that if someone keeps Jesus' commandments, He will manifest Himself to them. The word *manifest* means reveal. Jesus will reveal Himself in the life of the saved person who is obeying Him.

My desire is that my family not only "starts" well but also finishes well. That means the more they are aware of Jesus in their lives, the better their walk with Him will be, and the less likely that they will drift away. Therefore, it is our desire that we learn obedience, which begins by utilizing our time as the Lord directs, both individually and as a family.

I have seen when I am obedient so are my children.

More Practical Examples

Respecting others is the next point on the vision statement. This is developed through spending time in the Word and learning to value people. Having families over for dinner provides excellent, supervised training opportunities where the children learn to show proper respect for others. We regularly have hospitality evenings because this use of my time is in accordance with my vision statement.

Learning self-discipline comes from Scripture teaching us boundaries of proper behavior. Our evening Bible time allows us to discuss the practical implementation of being self-disciplined. As you are beginning to observe, our family Bible time targets many areas on my vision statement. Bible time is a bargain in time usage because of its multiplicity of applications. In addition, I spend time every week having an individual meeting with each child. This allows me to have input into their lives concerning their self-discipline—or lack of it. Then as the children grow older, they will have greater freedom and opportunity to exercise self-control while succeeding or failing within boundaries.

Loving children involves being around them. Since our children are no longer young, we enjoy being around families with little ones. Spending time with others is then consistent with our vision statement. As we fellowship together, our children's love of children deepens. Here again, time spent fellowshipping with other families is meeting more than one of the goals on my vision statement.

Holiness is learned by spending time in the Word, engaging in discussions as a family, and exercising good choices. To be holy means to be sanctified or set apart. We desire that our children learn that we are to live in the world, but our hearts are not to be for the world, but for things above. "Set your affection on things above, not on things on the earth"

(Colossians 3:2). Therefore, the activities that we spend our time on must not be the world's activities. "Ye adulterers and adulteresses, know ye not that the friendship of

> I meet too many men who ignore their families to focus on a ministry. Last month, a former pastor of ours stepped down because his oldest son rebelled— wrong focus/priority.

the world is enmity with God? whosoever therefore will be a friend of the world is the enemy of God" (James 4:4). How we spend our time greatly impacts whether our families will have a desire for the world or the things of the Lord.

Most families want their children to find God's spouse for them in a God-glorifying fashion, and the best book on this is the Bible. As we read God's Word, we discuss all aspects of life to include how God brings two people together. We talk about this at mealtime and family discussions. I see this time as well invested in the future of my children. After arming them with a heart knowledge of the process, my time will be needed, because my children will be sharing their questions, issues, concerns, joys, excitement, and plans with me.

A Few More Examples

To teach my children to be ambassadors for Christ means having them with me whenever possible. They see firsthand my interactions with those with whom we come in contact. They see how I delight in telling others of the One Who died for us. They see how I dress and act out of respect for our Lord and those we meet. Once again, this impacts my time.

There are several more aspects of my vision statement, but I have given you enough examples that I think you can observe how that vision statement impacts my time. Therefore, to wrap up this section, I am going to move to the last point in my vision statement.

For my children to be God's ambassadors, they must be free to follow the Lord. To be free, they must not be slaves to debt or the bank. This goal takes a great deal of my time. I help my children learn to manage their finances. I discuss the vision of their freedom from debt and why it is important. In addition, I encourage them to begin entrepreneurial businesses as teens, working and saving for the future. In this process, I am their encourager and consultant, so I spend many hours talking with them about equipment, quotes, how to tackle a job, and how to be successful.

> *I am free from mone- tary debt but sometimes feel a slave to my over-commit- ments.*

For us, God has clearly led that our children would not attend college. One of the reasons for this is because many people are slaves to their college loans. Having my children home during the usual college years, without a doubt, impacts my time as I continue to disciple them and advise them in their business ventures. Our children have owned the goal of being debt free to include even major purchases such as houses and vehicles. So far, our oldest two sons have purchased their homes debt free, and the younger three have that vision as well. (For more on this, see Resources at the back of this book for information on *Preparing Sons to Provide for a Single-Income Family.*)

Are We Asking Permission?

There is an old saying I heard for years: "It is easier to ask forgiveness than to ask permission." Is that our philosophy? Would we rather have our own way with our time and then ask forgiveness later when it doesn't work out very well? Or would we rather seek His direction early on? If time is wasted, second by second, minute by minute, hour by hour, day by day, week by week, month by month, and year by year, there is no reclaiming lost ground. It becomes too late for anything but regrets and sorrow. There are no regrets when our time is surrendered to Jesus. He will make the most of what we have to offer. We must seek Him daily in prayer for direction as we implement the vision He has given us.

As you can see by reading through my vision statement, it has had a very real and practical impact on the way I have spent my time through the years. It isn't enough just to avoid wasting time, but our time must be spent so as to edify and build up our families. The emphasis is on spending our time in a manner consistent with our vision statement. Jesus said that to avoid temptation, we must watch and pray. The world is full of enticements and temptations to pull us off course. To stay on the proper heading, we need a vision from the Lord, and we must pray and make decisions consistent with it.

My vision statement sets the course for my life and directs my time usage. It helps me redeem my time and to number my days. It gives me peace that when I choose to forgo an activity to instead spend family time in the Word, I am making a good decision about my time. It helps me make decisions on how to invest the time I have available because it is a guide to what the Lord has indicated is important in my family's lives. It is a key aspect of the stewardship and management of my time.

Time for the Word

If a Christian man chooses to manage his time, he must begin by looking to the One Who actually owns that time—the Lord Jesus Christ. How can I know what to spend my time on if I am not seeking that direction from my Savior? How will I have peace when there are time pressures in my life, if I'm not close to the One Who gives peace? In the midst of days that seem too full already, it is needful for us to invest time in our number-one priority in life—spiritual growth in Christ. That investment will pay huge dividends in our time management and our ability to cope with time pressure.

I want to help you come to a realization that time in the Word is important for every aspect of our daily lives and our family's lives, not just our time management. In addition, if we determine that we are going to spend time in the Word, when in the day will we fit it in? These are important details that relate to time for the Word.

"My husband's biggest issue with time management when it comes to spiritual headship is in a family Bible time. He desires to do it, and we do it off and on, but his work hours are late. When he gets home we always have dinner to eat and the children to get to bed."

Perhaps this comment represents what is typical of Christian men and the reality of time in the Word with their families. They know it is beneficial, they want to make it fit into their days, they may be successful occasionally, but the sad truth is that life pushes it out.

Marching with the Ants?

One morning as Teri and I were on our daily morning exercise and fellowship walk, she asked, "Did you see that huge ant trail you just stepped on?" I told her I hadn't been aware of the ants, but I made a mental note to watch for them after we turned around to head home. When we returned, I finally saw them, and she was right. There were so many ants moving together that it looked like a black line stretched across the ten-foot-wide sidewalk. I stopped for a minute just to watch them and mused out loud, "I wonder where they are going?" We started walking again, and to my surprise, about thirty feet down the hill, here was the same ant trail crossing the sidewalk again. I could see how they had traveled down the edge of the sidewalk and were going back to the other side again.

To an ant with its short legs, that extra twenty feet back and forth across the sidewalk would represent a significant amount of wasted time and effort. If they only could have had the vantage point that I had and have seen how much time and effort they were wasting when they could have gone straight down the one edge of the sidewalk. They were just following the guy in front, doing what he did, and going where he was going, but there was great waste in the process. In a similar fashion, I'm confident that the Lord, from His heavenly perspective, would say most Christian dads today are wasting significant amounts of time and energy. There is much unnecessary effort being expended on fruitless, temporal activities while things like being in the Word individually and as a family, which have eternal value, are left untouched. This might be an example:

> *"My husband is a volunteer firefighter and EMT. He considers this a ministry and spends time each week going on calls. He also helps the coaches with our son's football team. My husband occasionally reads the Bible to our two children and me, but this is when I ask him to. My husband is a wonderful provider, protector, and time manager—he accomplishes so much and stays pretty well caught up on his home projects, but he has never seemed to know how to be a spiritual leader in our home. He has always been supportive of my desires to train the children spiritually and to homeschool our children. He sets such a good example for our children in so many ways—as a very hard worker, faithful to all commitments."*

While this father has accomplished what the world would see as being a good father and time manager, what is he neglecting? It reminds me of this verse: "For what shall it profit a man, if he shall gain the whole world, and lose his own soul?" (Mark 8:36). What about the souls of his children?

A Tithe of Time?

One thing the world could benefit from is a perpetual energy machine. That would be a machine that created more energy than it used to produce it. The Bible is the closest thing I have found to that. Let me explain. On average I spend forty-five minutes in the morning for my personal Bible time, forty-five minutes in the evening for family Bible time, and ten minutes reading Scripture to Teri before we fall asleep. That is one hundred minutes a day out of the roughly 1,000 minutes I am awake. That is about 10 percent of my time, and it might be called a tithe. I didn't plan it that way, and until I ran the numbers just now, I wasn't aware of that. However, I have found I can't outdo God. Just like what He does with a monetary tithe, He gives back to me in time far more than I give to Him.

I spoke with a brother in Christ on the phone over the weekend and was encouraging him in being consistent in the Word every day. He admitted he has found that his days are so much more peaceful and productive when he has read his Bible in the morning before starting his day. He wasn't saying he read Scripture so his days would go better, but he read because he wanted fellowship with Jesus, and hearing from His Word every day was key to that. The end result is that our days do go much better. Even when a day is filled with problems, we can have peace in the midst of the storm.

> *"My husband is stressed most of the time. He won't allow himself to have time with his family when he is not working. His employer blows up quite often on employees, which causes extreme stress. Because my husband isn't in God's Word, he doesn't have the armor to see and fight the spiritual enemy. I love the Lord and the husband He gave me. I long to serve the Lord more as a family in every area of our lives."*

What would happen in this man's life and in the lives of his family if he began spending time in the Word personally and leading his family in Bible reading on a daily basis? Would he be able to deal with the stress? Would he be able to fight the spiritual battles? Would he be able to manage his time and have time with his family?

Directs My Time

When I'm in God's Word every day it is amazing how the Lord directs my time through His Word. He reminds me to spend my time on profitable things that edify others. "Let us therefore follow after the things which make for peace, and things wherewith one may edify another" (Romans 14:19). Then when there is a need to encourage a brother, I remind myself that this is a priority, and the Lord will manage the other demands on my time. When I'm working on a project such as writing this book, there have been a myriad of occasions when a child has come into my office with something that he wanted to run by me. God's Word encourages me of my vital priority of raising my children in the nurture and admonition of the Lord (Ephesians 6:4). I don't have to feel guilt or frustration and time pressure when I use my time consistently with His Word. I know I'm just being obedient.

Promotes Spiritual Growth

In conversations with people through the years, many times I have heard someone say something to me like, "What a blessing it must be to have been raised in a Christian home." Then they go on to say how they are a first-generation Christian. To their surprise, I explain that I wasn't saved until I was twenty-four years old and was definitely not raised in a Christian home. I share how Teri tells others that once I started having a personal time of Bible reading every day, she saw real spiritual growth in my life. God's Word is the stimulant for that growth. "As newborn babes, desire the sincere milk of the word, that ye may grow thereby: If so be ye have tasted that the Lord *is* gracious" (1 Peter 2:2-3).

Throughout this book, I share examples of spiritual growth that have occurred because of my Bible reading, how it has impacted my time, and how it has changed my thinking regarding time usage. A side note is in order. Please understand when I share personal examples, I'm NOT saying, "Look at how good I am." We have found through the years that people relate to personal examples, and that is why we include them. Anything good in me is a result of Jesus Christ when I yield to

His grace. That is what is so encouraging about being a follower of the Lord. I'm saying, "Look, if He can do that with even me, think about what He can do with you!"

Now let me give you an example of spiritual growth and how it has helped me even in the business world. When we started our family's home business, Communication Concepts, we needed to establish a pricing policy for how we would mark up the printing that we were brokering. The common practice I observed in the industry, and even among Christians in business, was that one customer would get one price and another would receive a different price for the same product and quantity. Pricing was mostly determined by what it took to get the business.

As I was trying to establish our pricing policy, one day I read in Proverbs 20:10: "Divers weights, *and* divers measures, both of them *are* alike abomination to the LORD." I saw that charging one person one price and another a different price is an abomination to the Lord. We wanted God's blessing on our business and certainly not His chastisement or curse. So we established a standardized pricing system for everyone. I then had peace that I was treating each customer fairly and could in good conscience look each one in the eye, knowing I wasn't taking advantage of him. In addition, it saved me time when quoting because I simply looked up on my chart the profit to charge based on the size of the order.

Despite continual pressure and stresses in my life from raising eight children, providing for them, and serving the Lord Jesus, I seldom feel like I am stressed. If I am awake in the night, which doesn't happen often, it is because the Lord has something He is telling me during those quiet moments. I attribute the peace in my heart to the spiritual growth and the relationship with Jesus that has developed in my life as a result of those hours I have spent in the Word through the years since my salvation.

Why Aren't We in the Word?

Over the last ten years since our ministry began, I have asked numerous dads if they read the Word individually and led family Bible time every day. Not very many men have responded "Yes" to both questions. I am sure there are men who do both daily, but sadly, I know the majority of "Christians" don't. Why not? Could the following be their justifications?

> They feel they and their families receive enough Bible teaching at church. *Possibly.*

> They feel their families already are dynamic followers of the Lord Jesus and additional Bible time is not necessary. *Very doubtful.*

> They don't even want to think about being in the Word every day because they are too busy with life and couldn't dream of adding one more thing. *Likely.*

I believe that men don't realize how critical being in the Word every day is to a man's whole life and certainly his time management. If they did realize it, I am confident that nothing could keep them from being in the Word. Instead of Bible time being one more burden in the day, men would come to understand how important reading Scripture every day is to a man's time management. It doesn't add to time pressures, but it will relieve them. Being in the Word daily is foundational as to how he spends every minute of his day that follows.

I've found that my mindset (priorities, values, goals, things I desire) is affected by how much time I spend listening to the world (TV, radio, paper, others and even some pastors) versus reading God's Word. The time in God's Word breaks down a worldly mindset—it's the only way to have the mind of Christ.

Our Highest Priority

Now that we see the importance of being in the Word every day, how do we make it happen? It will only happen if it is the high priority that it has to be. Good intentions are great, but it is actually fulfilling those intentions that matters.

As busy as you are, think about how many meals you have missed eating recently. When I have asked men to raise their hands during sessions inquiring how many of them were so busy that they had missed a meal in the last seven days, there are few, if any, hands that go up. Why? With all the busyness, people still find time to eat because it is a very high priority.

The reality is that although we seldom skip feeding our flesh, it is common to be too busy to feed ourselves and our families the Word of God. Doesn't this reflect our real priorities and highlight the war raging between the flesh and the Spirit?

I often ask the question, "Which is more important—the body or the spirit?" Anyone thinking about this will respond, "The spirit." The body will live eighty to a hundred years, but the spirit will live for eternity in either heaven or hell. It becomes obvious which one is the most important to feed properly. Remember the dad I mentioned earlier who said he had led his children to hell? He did not feed their spirits and bring them "up in the nurture and admonition of the Lord" (Ephesians 6:4).

I've challenged many men who struggle in being consistent with Bible time to make the commitment that they would not eat a bite of food for twenty-four hours any time they missed having their personal or family Bible time. They tell me it works wonders to keep a person faithful. If you want to be successful in being in the Word consistently, this will work.

There is a war between the flesh and the Spirit, and when it comes to being in the Word, the flesh is winning in the majority of homes. Once the choice is made to put time in the Word as the priority that it must be, you will be successful in having personal and family Bible time every day.

Real Life Challenges

As a young engineer early in my corporate career when there was tremendous time pressure at work, there was significant temptation in my heart to leave early for work instead of spending time in the Word. From discussions with other believers, when life gets very busy, one of the first things to be eliminated is time in the Word. However, when life is hectic and pressure-driven, that is when we should be in the Word more than anything else. At those moments, we desperately need to hear God's calming words of wisdom—a balm for our pressure-ridden souls, soothing music for our ears, and light to find the way for our obstacle-strewn paths. We will see how little our human efforts mean and be reminded of how the power of the Lord will far surpass our meager attempts.

When God called Gideon, what was he doing? Gideon was threshing wheat in a winepress to conceal it from the Midianites. He was hiding out of fear. What did an angel of the Lord say to him? ". . . The LORD *is* with thee, thou mighty man of valour" (Judges 6:12). How could the angel call Gideon a mighty man of valor when he was hiding and apparently fearful? It was because all that is needed for a cowardly person to be a mighty man of valor is to add the strength and power of the Lord to his life, just as in Gideon's life. Take a time-pressured, burdened dad struggling in life, give him anointing and direction from the Lord Jesus, couple that with obedience, and he will have productivity in exchange for floundering. "So shall my word be that goeth forth out of my mouth: it shall not return unto me void, but it shall accomplish that which I please, and it shall prosper *in the thing* whereto I sent it" (Isaiah

55:11). We will have time and the ability to do what the Lord says must be done when we only had time pressures previously.

When men are too busy to be in the Word personally and lead their families in the Word, it becomes a ripe opportunity for Jesus to show Himself mighty in multiplying their time—if only they would repent. That is a blessed season for God to get the glory instead of a man being proud of his accomplishments. Paul understood this perfectly. Paul felt that his thorn in the flesh was a hindrance to his ministry and asked the Lord to remove it. But He responded with, ". . . My grace is sufficient for thee: for my strength is made perfect in weakness. . ." (2 Corinthians 12:9). Paul's answer was: ". . . Most gladly therefore will I rather glory in my infirmities, that the power of Christ may rest upon me" (2 Corinthians 12:9).

Several years ago there was a time when the "plate" of things I was responsible for was so full, you couldn't tell there was a "plate." I had eight children, a ministry that required travel, a home business where we developed custom software, and I was pastoring our small start-up church. For some reason every time we had a ministry trip, we would be in the final stages of delivering software to our customer. Crisis after crisis would come along, and every second of the day was critical. I was not tempted to skip personal or family Bible time because I have learned through the years that I am absolutely dependent on God's grace and wisdom to make it through times like those.

I remember a time when our customer was testing the software prior to final acceptance, and they found a major bug. The more we dug into it, the worse it appeared to be, perhaps even requiring a major rewriting of code in an already very complex section. It would be impossible to rewrite that section, debug, test, and still meet the committed delivery date. However, as we cried out to the Lord, He revealed the perfect solution to the problem with one line of code. We have had something similar happen not once, but many times, and because of this, our determination grows to spend our time where God directs and trust Him with all the rest. God is ALWAYS faithful, but He does require our obedience. "Jesus answered and said unto him, If a man love me, he will keep my words: and my Father will love him, and we will come unto him, and make our abode with him" (John 14:23).

> I am also a computer programmer, but I have not trusted in the Lord at times. When I found a major bug like this once, I worked all night, slept about three hours, skipped Bible, and worked more. The problem just got worse. I finally gave up, prayed, read the Bible, and was able to solve the problem in about 10 minutes. Why did I skip God until the end?

Do we desire to be free from time pressures and to manage our time wisely? We won't receive these blessings in our own efforts and wisdom. We must acknowledge that we can't possibly get everything done that we think needs to be done in our strength. We can embrace the difficulties and pressure as opportunities for God to show Himself strong in our weakness. We begin by doing the right thing. "This book of the law shall not depart out of thy mouth; but thou shalt meditate therein day and night, that thou mayest observe to do according to all that is written therein: for then thou shalt make thy way prosperous, and then thou shalt have good success" (Joshua 1:8). The right thing for a believer, bought and paid for by Jesus Christ, is being in the Word, individually and as a family every day, regardless of whether or not we think we are too busy.

I Have to Warn You

When we built a house to make more room for our ministry, we put tile down on the whole main floor. We found it was less expensive than carpet if we ignored the cost to install it

> I used to watch football for hours and hours—Saturday, Sunday, Monday, and Thursday. What a waste.

since we would be doing that ourselves. It was a real learning experience for all involved. One lesson we learned too late was never to use a pencil to mark the tile before a cut. It turns out that removing pencil marks from tile is a very difficult, if not impossible, job. We would have been so grateful to the store that sold us the tile if they had warned us not to use a pencil on top of the tile to mark it.

In the same way, I have to warn you of something I have learned through the years. I share this brother to brother, and some may not like me for it, but I have to tell you upfront. If you watch TV, you are far, far, far more likely to fail in having daily time in the Word than those who don't watch TV.

It isn't difficult to understand why the TV is such a hindrance to being in the Word. Who doesn't like to be entertained? You sit down, put your feet up, and get comfortable, while your mind and eyes are occupied for some period of time. It is addicting, and that is why almost every American household has a television, and it is on most of the time.

> The Israelites were told to have nothing to do with pagan nations. Balaam convinced Balak's people to mix with Israel which resulted in the Israelites compromising and disobeying God.
> Can we please God while mixing with Hollywood? No!

I found over twenty years ago that it was a struggle to be consistent being in the Word while we were still watching television. Once we gave up TV and movies, being in the Word every day was a victory. "For the LORD thy God walketh in the midst of thy camp, to deliver thee, and to give up thine enemies before thee; therefore shall thy camp be holy: that he see no unclean thing in thee, and turn away from thee" (Deuteronomy 23:14). Could anyone consider general programming and many commercials to be holy? We are not to bring something unclean into our homes. Our homes are to be holy so that we can welcome His presence.

One dad e-mailed me and was very frustrated at his failed attempts to be in the Word every day with his family. I asked him if he had a "beast"—that is what I call a TV—because it will gobble up God's Word and our precious time. He said, "Yes, but we only watch the good shows." I questioned whether there was such a thing as good shows on general programming, and told him that he would most likely struggle as long as he had his beast. Three months later he wrote and told me that he had gotten rid of his television, and now they were able to be consistent in the Word.

> Would you feel comfortable with Jesus sitting on the couch with you to watch TV? Probably not. So if Jesus is really in your heart, why have a TV?

I have pleaded with many dads through the years to get rid of their beast and its soul-polluting, time-gobbling influence on their lives. You would think someone was trying to convince them to cut off their right arms by the struggle I see as a response to my encouragement.

It is because of the addicting, wicked pull away from the Lord that the Israelites were told to destroy the images of the foreign gods and all their pictures when they conquered other nations. "Then ye shall drive out all the inhabitants of the land from before you, and

> Second only to trusting the Lord for salvation, getting rid of the beast was the best decision I have ever made because it freed up everyone to be in the Word. Another thought. Do not wean yourself from the TV. Just cold turkey remove it.

destroy all their pictures, and destroy all their molten images, and quite pluck down all their high places" (Numbers 33:52). The rudimentary pictures God warned them about are nothing compared to the "moving pictures" of today. The things of the world are a snare to our souls and precious time. I share this brother to brother and would encourage each to strongly consider my words. Your family will be eternally grateful—once they get over the withdrawal.

Other Activities

You may find that there are family activities that add to time pressure and will conflict with time in the Word. When my two oldest sons, Nathan and Christopher, were young, they were in Little League baseball. Between practices and games, we found that our evening time was spent at the Little League field from March through August. The Lord began speaking to my heart that we were wasting our time on something that gave worldly pleasure as opposed to what would feed their souls. I presented individually to each boy the need for that to be their last season of baseball because it was too high of a price. I'm so grateful that the boys both agreed to follow me. If they hadn't been able to concur, they still would have had to quit, but it made it much better to have their support.

Do you have activities that are at war against time in the Word? It can be difficult to break away from them. There may be pressure from your friends, your family, and your children— even those who are Christians. You will find it easier if you decide up front that you don't care what men say. "But as we were allowed of God to be put in trust with the gospel, even so we speak; not as pleasing men, but God, which trieth our hearts" (1 Thessalonians 2:4). Joshua 24:15 says, ". . . but as for me and my house, we will serve the LORD." May we be men of God and from this day forward serve our God with our time, and not the gods of the nations. You will be freed from non-edifying activities, have the peace associated with spending time in the Word, and enjoy a closer walk with your Lord.

What Has Worked for Us

With over twenty years of experience having personal and family Bible time, it might be helpful for me to share some practices that have worked for us and have become stable blocks in our schedule. My personal time in the Word is always the first thing I do after getting dressed. That way there is nothing else to distract me, and it has worked well for all those years.

We have tried having our family Bible time both in the mornings and in the evenings, but the evening time has been most effective. Let me explain why, because our reasons for preferring the evening for family Bible could be the reasons you prefer the morning.

In the morning, we would have family Bible time at 6:25 a.m., allowing a half hour for it before I left for work. The morning was good in that there were few interruptions. However, we always had to end by seven o'clock so I could leave for work. Even if we were having a good discussion, I would have to break it off. The evenings were then open for family time, but it was easy for me to get involved in other activities and not spend time with the family. We also found morning family Bible time a lesser preference because I had to get up early enough to have both individual and family Bible time before work, and we ended up with double Bible time in the morning and nothing in the evening.

When we switched to having family Bible in the evening, we found it was a wonderful use of that time. Right after dinner cleanup is finished and before the family begins other projects, we gather in the living room for Bible time. I have discovered that if I tackle my highest priority first, it will always get done.

Next to the beast, the next biggest Bible-time wrecker is an inconsistent bedtime and rising time. Being rested is critical to being in the Word daily, while being too tired is often an excuse offered for not being in the Word. If a dad needed to be awake and alert in the evening to attend a special appointment where he would be given a million dollars, we all know he would do what he needed to do to be there on time. We accomplish what is important to us. We can choose to have a scheduled time to go to bed and get up in the morning. We must be sure it gives us enough sleep each night so that we will be able to consistently be in the Word with our families and be alert. It is a simple thing, and it will work.

The Spiritual Leader Leads Bible Time

It is very common for homeschool and Christian school children to have some Bible coursework to do every day. Should that suffice for your child's Bible teaching, and is it then not necessary for Dad to lead family Bible time? Wouldn't that be a great way to save Dad's time?

"Since I am a homeschool mom, my husband knows that the children are getting in-depth Bible, and he feels that is an area he is ill-equipped for. He has been a Christian for four years, and I for nine. I think he feels I am better qualified . . . UGHH . . . I know his heart feels the pressure of wanting to do something to lead our family but not knowing how to do it. He is an amazing man who loves us deeply, and his heart has changed so much since he has come to read the Word daily."

Scripture teaches that Dad is to be the spiritual leader of the home. "And, ye fathers, provoke not your children to wrath: but bring them up in the nurture and admonition of the Lord"

(Ephesians 6:4). If Mom, or someone else, is teaching and over-seeing the children's Bible instruction even under the father's direction, that person becomes the leader. The children will go to them with their questions, and they will be seen as the spiritual authority. We don't want that for our family.

In cases like the example we just read of here, I would encourage the dad to start family Bible time. I believe he will discover he is fully qualified because of his heart for the Lord Jesus, and that he will be abundantly blessed in the process. He doesn't have to have all of the answers, just a heart for leading his family and learning with them. I recently spoke to a man who said something like this to me: "Wow, why didn't I know the joys of family Bible time before this? I thought I had to have all the answers to have a Bible time with my children, but I don't. We discuss verses as a family, and we are all growing together. It is beautiful."

Family Bible time and its importance to Christian families was such a burden on my heart, that I did a 2 CD resource called *Feed My Sheep: A Practical Guide to Daily Family Bible Time.* The CDs will equip you with information on how to have Bible time with your family, along with laying the foundation for how absolutely necessary it is to your family's spiritual growth. Please see Resources at the back of this book for more information.

What about the Exceptions?

Oftentimes as we are traveling, a father will tell me that he can't have consistent family Bible time because of a multitude of time-related reasons. After a brief exchange with him, it becomes clear whether it is a deep desire of the dad's heart to be feeding his family the Word of God, or whether the lack of time is just an excuse. The one is desperately

We had to do ours over webcam when I was in Florida for training.

seeking new and creative ways to spiritually feed his flock, and the other is looking for good excuses.

"He does lead us in Bible reading on most evenings that we are home as a family, but when something comes up that we have to be gone for, and it is bedtime before we get home, then he does not."

I learned firsthand how easy it was to let family Bible time slide for one reason or another, and being out late was one of the top excuses. However, I found great freedom in making a commitment that we would have family Bible time, every day, no matter what. I discovered that we could forget to have our Bible time in the afternoon before a conference, get to our hotel at 11:00 p.m., be exhausted, have to be up at 6:00 a.m. to be at the conference or driving, and still have family Bible before we went to bed. We weren't any worse off for the lesser amount of sleep, and I am convinced we profited from that time spent in the Word.

I always come back to it being an issue between a dad and his God. ". . . Thus saith the Lord GOD unto the shepherds; Woe *be* to the shepherds of Israel that do feed themselves! should not the shepherds feed the flocks? Ye eat the fat, and ye clothe you with the wool, ye kill them that are fed: *but* ye feed not the flock" (Ezekiel 34:2-3). I'm sure those shepherds in Ezekiel 34 were busy and had good reasons for not feeding the flocks, but I also see clearly that God didn't accept their reasons. He chastened them anyway. "Thus saith the Lord GOD; Behold, I *am* against the shepherds; and I will require my flock at their hand, and cause them to cease from feeding the flock; neither shall the shepherds feed themselves any more; for I will deliver my flock from their mouth, that they may not be meat for them" (Ezekiel 34:10). I believe many dads are under God's chastisement for not doing what God has called them to do regardless of how busy they are. Is it possible that some of that chastening is in the form of stress and time pressure? May each man seek his Lord's face and be obedient. I think often Satan gets far too much credit for hindering people when the fact is that we just make poor decisions and are disciplined for them.

It's a War

"No man that warreth entangleth himself with the affairs of *this* life; that he may please him who hath chosen him to be a soldier" (2 Timothy 2:4). The flesh is lazy and self-seeking, and we must be on guard. "For they that are after the flesh do mind the things of the flesh; but they that are after the Spirit the things of the Spirit" (Romans 8:5). There are more than enough excuses for every day of the year to explain why we are too busy to be in the Word ourselves and lead our families in Bible time. Everyone but the Lord Jesus might agree that there isn't time. However, the only One Who matters says, ". . . Feed my sheep" (John 21:16). He has spoken clearly that we must do it.

When we choose obedience to His Word, we will reap the benefits concerning our time management. We are learning the mind of Christ regarding what is important and what isn't, and that certainly affects how we choose to spend our time. We find out what the Lord wants His children to invest their time in and what He has for them to avoid.

Finally, time in the Word allows us to grow spiritually so that when we have time pressure, we will be able to rest in the Lord. We can experience the reality of His strength in our weakness. We will be men who have given their time to the Lord Jesus for His use. We are redeeming our time and learning to number our days.

Bringing Home the Bacon

As we evaluate how a man manages his time, providing for his family will certainly take up a significant portion of most days. The job he has, the hours he works, and the commute, all will impact a man's time. The ability to manage the working part of a day will be important as a man manages his overall time and deals with time pressure he faces. In considering the management of work time, there is often little that a man can do to affect those hours. However, there are aspects of his spiritual walk with the Lord Jesus Christ that will have a huge influence on how a man deals with his work time and any pressure that time brings to him. Some will wonder about the possibility of a home business as a solution to providing for a family and being better able to manage time.

Who Is the Provider?

God has called the husband to be the provider. "But if any provide not for his own, and specially for those of his own house, he hath denied the faith, and is worse than an infidel" (1 Timothy 5:8). Providing for a family takes a large amount of time, can be a source of great pressure, and can easily take the joy out of life. That is likely the result when a man is focusing on his ability to provide and not on the Lord's provision. The more we take our eyes off of the Lord and onto the needs of life, the more it is possible that we will sink. When Peter began to walk on the water, it was when he looked at the wind's affect on the waves that he began to sink. "But when he saw the wind boisterous, he was afraid; and beginning to sink, he cried, saying, Lord, save me" (Matthew 14:30). Are our eyes fastened on our Lord, or are we looking at the waves around us?

Each is told in Romans 12:3 "... not to think of *himself* more highly than he ought to think...." Who do we believe is ultimately responsible for feeding our families? If we think it is ourselves, then are we possibly thinking of ourselves more highly than we ought to think? If we are servants of the Most High God, isn't it the Master's responsibility to provide? Of course! Then what is our responsibility? We are to be busy about the Master's work.

We read: "But seek ye first the kingdom of God, and his righteousness; and all these things shall be added unto you" (Matthew 6:33). What is Jesus referring to that will be added unto us? He has told us in 6:25, "Therefore I say unto you, Take no thought for your life, what ye shall eat, or what ye shall drink; nor yet for your body, what ye shall put on. Is not the life more than meat, and the body than raiment?" The Lord is saying He provides for the sparrows, and He will provide for us if we will seek His kingdom first.

Does that mean that we all quit our secular work and head off to the jungle to be missionaries? No—well, not unless the Lord tells us to. We apply that verse by making our relationship with Jesus our highest priority. When we are abiding in a close relationship with Jesus, He will use us in our employment, whether secular or ministry related, for the glory of His name.

"Whether therefore ye eat, or drink, or whatsoever ye do, do all to the glory of God" (1 Corinthians 10:31). We give our best in whatever vocation the Lord has placed us. I must add a caveat to that statement. I've known some dads who have shared with me that they were working for a business that is contrary to the kingdom of God, and they considered it a great mission field. We can be unequally yoked by working for an ungodly company. Some quick examples of businesses contrary to the kingdom of God would be those associated with gambling, alcohol, or tobacco. These particular businesses enslave their customers. "But whoso shall offend one of these little ones which believe in me, it were better for him that a millstone were hanged about his neck, and *that* he were drowned in the depth of the sea" (Matthew 18:6). Brother to brother, I would encourage you to look for an opportunity to change jobs.

> 15 years ago I was looking for a job and about 60% of the openings I could not apply for (i.e. cable TV). How can I work for a company whose goal is to provide R-rated content (and worse) to the home? I could not.

Might Never Be Enough Time

Some dads are caught on a treadmill running for all they are worth, and no matter how hard they try, there is not enough time or money. The Lord has called us to work hard, but it would seem that the efforts of many are just being poured out on the ground so we work longer and harder. Do you ever feel that way? Here is an example:

"My children and I believe that Dad is a workaholic. His top priority is his job no matter what is going on with the family. This has been the case for many years whether or not he has had control over his hours of work. Due to his consistent absence, not just physically, all family responsibilities are left to Mom. Often, it's just too much work and not enough family relationship time."

Deuteronomy 28 presents both the blessings of obeying the Lord and the curses for disobedience. I believe we have seen the blessings on Christian families and our country for two hundred years. However, we are now headed down the path of experiencing God's curses as listed below.

As you read, ask yourself whether you prefer the blessings or the curses. Do you have these blessings on your labors? I can tell you, it is a wonderful thing. I have never deserved the way He has blessed my family. I don't obey Him to get a blessing. I obey Him because He is my Lord and Savior. It would be enough to be His child; yet, He heaps blessing upon blessing when we obey Him.

> 1 "And it shall come to pass, if thou shalt hearken diligently unto the voice of the LORD thy God, to observe *and* to do all his commandments which I command thee this day, that the LORD thy God will set thee on high above all nations of the earth:"
>
> 2 "And all these blessings shall come on thee, and overtake thee, if thou shalt hearken unto the voice of the LORD thy God."
>
> 3 "Blessed *shalt* thou *be* in the city, and blessed *shalt* thou *be* in the field."
>
> 4 "Blessed *shall be* the fruit of thy body, and the fruit of thy ground, and the fruit of thy cattle, the increase of thy kine, and the flocks of thy sheep."
>
> 5 "Blessed *shall be* thy basket and thy store." [Our income and savings.]
>
> 6 "Blessed *shalt* thou *be* when thou comest in, and blessed *shalt* thou *be* when thou goest out."

7 "The LORD shall cause thine enemies that rise up against thee to be smitten before thy face: they shall come out against thee one way, and flee before thee seven ways."

8 "The LORD shall command the blessing upon thee in thy storehouses, and in all that thou settest thine hand unto; and he shall bless thee in the land which the LORD thy God giveth thee."

9 "The LORD shall establish thee an holy people unto himself, as he hath sworn unto thee, if thou shalt keep the commandments of the LORD thy God, and walk in his ways."

10 "And all people of the earth shall see that thou art called by the name of the LORD; and they shall be afraid of thee."

11 "And the LORD shall make thee plenteous in goods, in the fruit of thy body, and in the fruit of thy cattle, and in the fruit of thy ground, in the land which the LORD sware unto thy fathers to give thee."

12 "The LORD shall open unto thee his good treasure, the heaven to give the rain unto thy land in his season, and to bless all the work of thine hand: and thou shalt lend unto many nations, and thou shalt not borrow."

13 "And the LORD shall make thee the head, and not the tail; and thou shalt be above only, and thou shalt not be beneath; if that thou hearken unto the commandments of the LORD thy God, which I command thee this day, to observe and to do *them*:" (Deuteronomy 28:1-13).

I believe all of the above is summarized by Jesus in Matthew 6:33: "But seek ye first the kingdom of God, and his righteousness; and all these things shall be added unto you."

The Curses for Disobedience

Now compare the blessings of obedience to the curses of disobedience, and it becomes clear why many today are wearing themselves out to feed their families. Understand, I'm not saying that all hardship is a result of chastening or a curse, but I do believe that it is very common. Note how there are far more consequences for disobedience than blessings for obedience.

15 "But it shall come to pass, if thou wilt not hearken unto the voice of the LORD thy God, to observe to do all his commandments and his statutes which I command thee this day; that all these curses shall come upon thee, and overtake thee:"

16 "Cursed *shalt* thou *be* in the city, and cursed *shalt* thou *be* in the field."

17 "Cursed *shall be* thy basket and thy store." [A man's income and savings!]

18 "Cursed *shall be* the fruit of thy body, and the fruit of thy land, the increase of thy kine, and the flocks of thy sheep."

19 "Cursed *shalt* thou *be* when thou comest in, and cursed *shalt* thou *be* when thou goest out."

20 "The LORD shall send upon thee cursing, vexation, and rebuke, in all that thou settest thine hand unto for to do, until thou be destroyed, and until thou perish quickly; because of the wickedness of thy doings, whereby thou hast forsaken me."

21 "The LORD shall make the pestilence cleave unto thee, until he have consumed thee from off the land, whither thou goest to possess it."

22 "The LORD shall smite thee with a consumption, and with a fever, and with an inflammation, and with an extreme burning, and with the sword, and with blasting, and with mildew; and they shall pursue thee until thou perish."

23 "And thy heaven that *is* over thy head shall be brass, and the earth that is under thee *shall be* iron."

24 "The LORD shall make the rain of thy land powder and dust: from heaven shall it come down upon thee, until thou be destroyed."

25 "The LORD shall cause thee to be smitten before thine enemies: thou shalt go out one way against them, and flee seven ways before them: and shalt be removed into all the kingdoms of the earth."

26 "And thy carcase shall be meat unto all fowls of the air, and unto the beasts of the earth, and no man shall fray *them* away."

27 "The LORD will smite thee with the botch of Egypt, and with the emerods, and with the scab, and with the itch, whereof thou canst not be healed."

28 "The LORD shall smite thee with madness, and blindness, and astonishment of heart:"

29 "And thou shalt grope at noonday, as the blind gropeth in darkness, and thou shalt not prosper in thy ways: and thou shalt be only oppressed and spoiled evermore, and no man shall save *thee.*"

30 "Thou shalt betroth a wife, and another man shall lie with her: thou shalt build an house, and thou shalt not dwell therein: thou shalt plant a vineyard, and shalt not gather the grapes thereof."

31 "Thine ox *shall be* slain before thine eyes, and thou shalt not eat thereof: thine ass *shall be* violently taken away from before thy face, and shall not be restored to thee: thy sheep *shall be* given unto thine enemies, and thou shalt have none to rescue *them*."

32 "Thy sons and thy daughters *shall be* given unto another people, and thine eyes shall look, and fail *with longing* for them all the day long: and *there shall be* no might in thine hand."

33 "The fruit of thy land, and all thy labours, shall a nation which thou knowest not eat up; and thou shalt be only oppressed and crushed alway:"

34 "So that thou shalt be mad for the sight of thine eyes which thou shalt see."

35 "The LORD shall smite thee in the knees, and in the legs, with a sore botch that cannot be healed, from the sole of thy foot unto the top of thy head."

36 "The LORD shall bring thee, and thy king which thou shalt set over thee, unto a nation which neither thou nor thy fathers have known; and there shalt thou serve other gods, wood and stone."

37 "And thou shalt become an astonishment, a proverb, and a byword, among all nations whither the LORD shall lead thee."

38 "Thou shalt carry much seed out into the field, and shalt gather *but* little in; for the locust shall consume it."

39 "Thou shalt plant vineyards, and dress *them*, but shalt neither drink *of* the wine, nor gather *the grapes*; for the worms shall eat them."

40 "Thou shalt have olive trees throughout all thy coasts, but thou shalt not anoint *thyself* with the oil; for thine olive shall cast *his fruit*."

41 "Thou shalt beget sons and daughters, but thou shalt not enjoy them; for they shall go into captivity."

42 "All thy trees and fruit of thy land shall the locust consume."

43 "The stranger that *is* within thee shall get up above thee very high; and thou shalt come down very low."

44 "He shall lend to thee, and thou shalt not lend to him: he shall be the head, and thou shalt be the tail." (Deuteronomy 28:15-44)
[Notice borrowing is a curse!]

Our country was founded under God and as a result has been blessed beyond measure. Sadly, our country has now turned from God, and we are beginning to see curse upon curse being manifested. And in reality, "Christian" families are merely following the same worldly path our country is trodding.

A Choice

The choice for each family is whether they will serve God with their time or serve something else. You cannot serve two masters. "No man can serve two masters: for either he will hate the one, and love the other; or else he will hold to the one, and despise the other. Ye cannot serve God and mammon" (Matthew 6:24). A family can have God's blessing if they will but choose to follow their God. God has said He will provide if we are obedient. I need to be clear. I'm not talking about a "name-it, claim-it" prosperity teaching. God calls us to work, casting our cares upon Him, and He says He will take care of us.

Dads are under great pressure, but that does not need to be the case. "Take therefore no thought for the morrow: for the morrow shall take thought for the things of itself. Sufficient unto the day *is* the evil thereof" (Matthew 6:34). We are told not to worry about tomorrow; therefore it is disobedience if we choose to do that.

God is not going to provide for whatever we might covet. "Ye ask, and receive not, because ye ask amiss, that ye may consume *it* upon your lusts" (James 4:3). If we have amassed large debt for selfish pleasure, we can expect to be on that "treadmill" for a very long time. If we are looking to the Lord to provide for our needs as we follow Him, we can count on Him being faithful.

The previous chapter about being in the Word individually and as a family was purposely placed before this chapter. The dad who is abiding in Jesus is not going to be feeling pressure. Once Dad begins to understand the mind of his God in relation to being a spiritual leader and making a living, so many things will fall into place. "Labour not for the meat which perisheth, but for that meat which endureth unto everlasting life, which the Son of man shall give unto you: for him hath God the Father sealed" (John 6:27). The inverse is true as well. Until he comes to that understanding, he likely will be under all sorts of pressure and waste time on things the Lord would not have him do. Where are you? Are you beginning to perceive how these pieces of a puzzle fit together?

An Example

"My husband is in law school, two hours away from home three nights a week. He also manages our small farm, as well as his family's farm. He also clerks for a local law firm three

days a week. We have six children with a seventh on the way. We have eliminated many, if not all, of the extras of life: sports, TV, etc. He does Bible study MOST days but not daily. We just barely make it through the necessities of life."

After reading this example, one might wonder whether this dad has really been called to law school. He has responsibility for his farm plus the family farm, which are probably responsibilities that won't change when he becomes a lawyer. The time away from home on school nights plus the part-time job as a clerk at a local law firm will eat up what little time this father has with his family. He is putting a high priority on family Bible time, but the difficulty his time choices are making on his family is evident. If the Lord wants him to become a lawyer, perhaps He will provide a way to let go of the farming, move closer to school, and temporarily live off a part-time income. I personally expect this father to soon begin reaping some of the curses of which we read, if he isn't reaping them already.

The Vital Priority

A father's vital priority will involve his family, as we find in Ephesians 6:4: "And, ye fathers, provoke not your children to wrath: but bring them up in the nurture and admonition of the Lord." Discipling our children is 100 percent consistent with seeking first the kingdom of God. But I ask you, which is easier, to go to work or to disciple your children? Most would agree that it is far easier to accomplish the tasks assigned to us at the job versus the discipleship of a child. Clearly, though, our work is merely "wood, hay, and stubble" in comparison to nurturing eternal souls. Raising our children to be dynamic followers of the Lord Jesus Christ must be the deep burden of our hearts. Because men are so easily distracted by their work, we must continually keep in mind our vital priority.

Many families are losing their children (even home-schooled ones!) to the world. There is much more involved to raising children than simply homeschooling them and bringing them to church. Teri and I share in *Keeping Our Children's Hearts: Our Vital Priority*, how we have kept the hearts of our children, avoiding rebellion. Please see Resources at the back of the book for more information.

What if my wife became so consumed with housework that she allowed the children to run wild all day? After waking up, she hurried to get started cleaning the house and didn't take time to read her Bible. She kept working all day, only stopping to go out to eat. Finally in the evening, she would relax, saying she deserved it, but still have no time for the children. Would I be pleased? That is how Mom sees it when Dad is consumed with work and doesn't own responsibility for discipling the children. Do we work to live or live to work? May the burden of our hearts be the bringing up of our children in the nurture and admonition of the Lord, and may we see work as just something we do to feed the family and pay the bills. May we have hearts given fully to the Lord Jesus and our families. I believe that as our priorities begin to change the time pressures will lessen as well.

Pressure of a Different Sort

Once you have put work in its proper priority, you can expect the possibility of a new kind of pressure. This will be pressure from others to make their priorities your priorities. As you begin to put your family first, others may criticize you. Here is an example from our recent Titus2 survey. This mom writes:

"There is a Christian, homeschool dad in the office who comes in at nine and leaves at four every day. He never ever takes any work home. He is very polite and loves his family. He has NO respect among his peers and NO testimony. We

see the cause of Christ in the office so inhibited by his behavior. You must imagine the pressure that puts on the other Christians in the office."

We are assuming that this man's designated work hours are nine to four, or his boss would not retain him as an employee. No doubt the other Christians in that office are putting pressure on this dad to work longer and conform. He is brave in his willingness to put his family first. The fact that he hasn't lost his job tells me that his boss values his work and isn't requiring him to work overtime. Obviously, this wife is not agreeing with the other dad's choice to put his family first. Frankly, I applaud this dad. I feel he is the one who has an eye on eternity and is willing to invest in his family and God's kingdom. I am confident that in twenty years, this dad will bear rich fruit in his family as a result of the tough choices he is making today. We can see that making the

19 years ago, shortly after our first child was born, my work situation got difficult. Projects were being cancelled, and there were constant layoffs. My project was "in jeopardy," and we were all informed we had to work 60-80 hours/week. God made it clear to me that this would result in the sacrifice of the family He gave me—not His will. I cried out to God, and then told my boss I would only work 40 hours/week, because of my priorities, and that if he felt it wasn't enough, he'd have to let me go. God blessed my decision. Not only did I keep my job, but I saw many others get burned out and destroy their families. It reinforced that I made the right decision. I relied on the Lord, obeyed Him, and He blessed. Results may not be seen for years (20?) until the children grow up, and fruit is apparent.

right choice often means that we will come under fire, perhaps even from other believers. The decision for each to make is Who/who we will serve with the most precious thing we have—our time. Can you make those difficult decisions?

Contrast the example we just read with the following one.

"This has been a source of conflict for us. My husband believes that loyalty to his employer is mandatory for continued income. I believe that continued neglect of relationships and spiritual leadership doesn't align with our priorities. Saying that family comes before work is empty after eighteen years and counting of absentee parenting. I long for my children to know what a two-parent household looks like in daily life. We operate as if I am a single parent. I am solely responsible for our six children's physical, educational, and spiritual needs. I hope that he will find his way home before it is too late to repair the missing relationships with his children."

Which Dad has his eye on eternity? Which one is trusting the Lord Jesus for His provision? Which one is blessing his wife and children by putting them ahead of his work? Which one is obediently following the Lord Jesus Christ with his life?

How to Make the Most of It

Next let's look at ways we can redeem the time related to work. One place to start is with the commute, and what can be done to redeem those hours. However, while trying to be efficient with that time, safety is the primary caution. To make better use of the commute and be injured in an accident because we weren't paying attention to traffic would not be a good tradeoff.

Living in Leavenworth, Kansas, while working in Kansas City, Missouri, afforded me the longest commute of any place we have lived. Commute traffic was light and fairly consistent. Barring bad weather, it took around fifty minutes each way. For years I was able to use a portion of my commute to memorize Scripture. "Thy word have I hid in mine heart, that I might not sin against thee" (Psalms 119:11). I wrote my verses on note cards using large letters, putting it on my dash. It was easy to read, and I could still see traffic. It took me much longer to memorize than it would have had I been at home without distractions, but I still memorized an amazing amount of Scripture during those years.

I also enjoyed listening to the Bible on CD. "But his delight *is* in the law of the LORD; and in his law doth he meditate day and night" (Psalms 1:2). Now I have an iPod, and I have found that it is helpful for listening to Scripture. Earphones are not a good idea during a commute because they would block out ambient sounds, including car horns. iPods, though, can be played easily over the car radio using inexpensive FM transmitters designed for that purpose.

> That's been a great blessing to me. I go through the entire Bible twice a year. Plus, I sing along to hymns, praise songs, and focus on a book or Psalms at times.
>
> My New Testament MP3 is only 18 hours. I could go through this in 2 weeks!!!

I would strongly encourage dads NOT to try to substitute listening to sermons while you drive for your daily personal time in the Word. Is not the Lord worthy of our undivided attention? "But thou, when thou prayest, enter into thy closet, and when thou hast shut thy door, pray to thy Father which is in secret; and thy Father which seeth in secret shall reward thee openly" (Matthew 6:6). Jesus tells us plainly that we should get where we can give the Father our undivided attention when we go to Him.

> I've found sermons are full of opinions. If I'm not grounded in Scripture, I end up listening to men and not to God and get pulled off track.

It is good to look for other ways we can redeem the commute time. Anything we can do safely while we drive is a bonus and frees our time later. The drive can be a beneficial time to plan and think about the needs of the family. I used to have a pocket recorder in the car that I "took notes" with while I drove. Make the drive home your unwinding time so that when you arrive, you are recharged and ready to begin your real job of leading your family and discipling your children.

A Warning

I would strongly encourage you to avoid a trap I fell into. I felt that it was important for me to listen to a secular talk show host with whom I agreed politically. He was very popular, provided political insight, and was highly entertaining. Sadly, his shows mocked those in authority and were often filled with sexual innuendos.

During that time, I found myself struggling greatly against impure thoughts. As hard as I tried, I could not shake myself of those thoughts. While crying out to the Lord, I became convicted about listening to that program. I thought certainly that show couldn't be the problem because I was an adult quite capable of casting out the bad and receiving the good. I was wrong. I finally surrendered to the Lord's leading and stopped listening to the show. I was soon free from those thoughts. Please don't make the same mistake I made. Don't listen to the world's carnal entertainment; it will affect your heart. Redeem the time with things that are edifying in the Lord Jesus.

> I've had a similar issue, but with a "better" entertainer/talk show host. My problem was that it changed my focus to the world, its ways, and its problems. It took my mind and focus off of God's kingdom and onto the kingdom of this world—Satan's realm.

Distance from Work

You might consider moving closer to work. If you value your time in light of eternity, saving even a half hour a day—being fifteen minutes closer to work—could pay eternal dividends. A half hour adds up to approximately 125 hours each year of extra time, which is the equivalent of about eight more days of usable time added to your life in just a year. Assuming the average family has three hours a night together, that is the same as Dad having an additional forty-two days more of evening time with his family over the course of a year. During twenty years of raising children, that computes to 840 days more of evening time with the children. That, to me, is priceless time. Remember our goal to learn to number our days. "So teach *us* to number our days, that we may apply *our* hearts unto wisdom" (Psalms 90:12).

I have spoken to many dads through the years who have told me, with happiness in their voices, that they are moving to the country. My heart sinks when they mention the added commute time, which often totals an extra hour or more a day. As they speak, I also think of all the additional farm responsibilities they will acquire that will demand their time. Then they say it will be worth it to have a place in the country. I wonder if the Lord will agree. If the dad has a job where he can work from home, "AMEN!" But I would plead with dads to count the greatest cost, and that is your time away from the family.

Minimizing Time Away

If our hearts are to be home with our families, we will do everything we can to be at home more. Some companies allow their employees to work from home for one or more days a week. If that is an option for you, take it, but be extremely careful to be diligent. If you can't have undisturbed time to be productive in your work, either you could find yourself out of a job altogether, or you could be, in essence, stealing time from your employer. Be zealous about doing the best you can to safeguard such a wonderful opportunity.

For years, at my corporate job, I worked through my lunch hour. I still came and left at the normal time, but it allowed me to get more done without having to stay late. I've noticed that some employees will take breaks through the day and spend time chatting with coworkers. Avoiding office talk enables us to get more accomplished in the day. The goal is to be a valuable asset to the company without having to take time away from the family.

If the workload can be managed without having to work through the lunch hour, and there is no option of going home early (by using flex hours, for example), then consider using lunchtime for things that take you or your wife's time at home. There were other years when I ran all the errands for the family during my lunch hour. I would have to bring a large cooler with me to work so I could make a trip to Sam's Club, but it saved precious family time. If I could complete the errand in my lunch hour, I would do it.

I also made family phone calls during lunch as well. If I needed insurance quotes or questions answered for home projects, they could all be made then. I didn't have time to go to lunch with coworkers this way, but it saved my "fellowship" time for those who were most important to me—my family.

Another way I utilized my lunch hour to gain time with my family was by exercising. At one job, the company provided shower and locker facilities that allowed employees to exercise during their hours at work. Despite the fact we lived in Florida and noon was beastly hot in the summer, I used that hour of time to take a run. With careful attention to managing my lunch hour, there was just enough time to get changed, run, shower, and be back to my desk at 1:00.

What about "Impossible" Jobs?

I know there are some jobs that make it very difficult to limit the time spent at work. However, I wonder if there is ever a job that the Lord would agree excuses a man from spending the time required to disciple the children. The question is, how serious is the dad about his responsibility?

"My husband is active duty with the US Army, and they own him. He gets up in time to read God's Word every morning, for which I am truly grateful. He likes to surf the Internet as soon as he's through with his time with the Lord. He's off to work usually around 6:30, so he often misses seeing the children in the morning. He does say a prayer with me before he leaves. He is usually home close to 6, but very often as late as 7-9. On average he has off two weekends a month, four days total. This means he works straight through for sometimes up to three weeks with no days off. This is wearing out our family. It is very difficult. Yes, God gives me strength, but so often I ask Him, 'Is this how it is supposed to be?'"

The following words are extremely difficult for me to write; please receive them in the spirit of love they are given. I'm not judging anyone, but sharing the hard facts of life regarding military service. Being in the military can pose serious threats to a man being the spiritual leader of his family, and no other job is like it. When a person is in the military, he is owned, as this wife writes, "by another." That is the simple truth, and Dad's time is not his time. He is a servant of the government, and his family comes second to "Uncle Sam." I have extensive experience with the military, having been in the service myself and having lived in a military community for two decades. Teri is the daughter of a retired Army officer, and we have had many friends who are career military.

I wholeheartedly believe that a man who chooses to stay in the military has to accept the fact that he can't lead his family spiritually in the same way he could if he were a civilian. That is why I have encouraged many men through the years to get out as soon as they have the opportunity. There are a host of men who will serve in the military, but you are the only one who can be a dad to your children.

What about the dad who has a crazy work schedule and is required to work long and unpredictable hours? If that is you, first critically evaluate your heart. I've known dads who use their work as an excuse to not be the dad God has called them to be. It is easier to have someone else tell you what to do at work than to be the one at home who is responsible for discipling the children. Could that be the case? I've known men who were unwilling to approach their bosses about a reduction in overtime and then made it sound like there was no option but to work that many hours each week.

What about an example where there is no hope to change the schedule or cut the work hours? Let's say a dad is a fireman, and he has twenty-four hours on followed by forty-eight off. What could he do? The first step is to see if he owns this responsibility for his family by looking at his days off. Is he spending time with his family? Does he lead the family in the Word every day that he is off? That is usually a great indicator of whether he is looking for an excuse or really has the right heart but has no idea how to make it work.

In addition to this dad discipling his family on his days off, he would then begin looking for creative ways to have family Bible time on the days he had to work. Are there possible hours when the family could go to the fire station and have family Bible time with Dad? I've seen families at our neighborhood fire station with Dad while he is on duty. If they can't go there, does Dad have any free time, even if it is unscheduled, where he could phone the family? If so, using a speakerphone, he could lead the Bible time almost as well as if he were at home. I've known military dads who have recorded Bible times ahead, and then Mom plays it to the family when he is away. A webcam or similar service can make family Bible time seem almost like Dad is right in the room with the family.

The alternatives are not as efficient or convenient as being home, but they are far better than not having Bible time at all, or even having Mom leading it. How committed are we to feeding our family the Word of God? Remember, when we are fulfilling the responsibilities that God has given us, He blesses our time. We will be far more productive when we are busy about His work.

Is a Home or Family Business the Answer?

I have spoken to many dads whose dream is to have a home business. A home business can be an exciting subject, but it is also very serious, not just a matter of "ten easy steps" to success. Is a home business right for you?

I am sure there are lots of resources telling dads just how they can have a home business and be their own boss. It sounds good. However, so many of those dreams turn into nightmares. That nightmare begins if Dad starts a home business but the Lord isn't directing. There are other times when He might have been calling the dad to a home business, but it just wasn't the time for the sending. This means that Dad gets ahead of the Lord, and therefore the pursuit isn't blessed. Families can end up emotionally drained and financially ruined. If those worst-case scenarios don't happen, Dad might end up a slave to the demands of the business with no time for the family.

Dads and moms will write to me and ask, "How did you leave corporate America and begin your family business Communication Concepts?" They are, in essence, asking for those "ten easy steps." There really isn't such a thing in my opinion. The closest would be: abide in Christ, love His Word, obey Him, and He will direct your paths. "In all thy ways acknowledge him, and he shall direct thy paths" (Proverbs 3:6). If we are His servants, then we are at His disposal. If the Lord Jesus feels we are more profitable to His kingdom by having a home business, then He will lead us that way when it is the proper time.

I am an electrical engineer and worked in engineering jobs for close to twenty years. For many of those years, it was on my heart to have a home business, but I had a good job with benefits that supported my family. I didn't feel God telling me it was time to quit my corporate work to start a home business. However, there came a time when He made it very clear that I was to pursue a home business because I was laid off of my corporate job with a severance package. Since it was the proper time, He made it crystal clear what He wanted me to do.

Could God Be Calling You to a Home or Family Business?

I would expect to see a number of things in the life of a man whom God is calling to a home business. First, I would expect to see that he has proven himself faithful to being daily in the Word individually and leading his family in it. Being in the Word daily gives a man sensitivity to the Lord's promptings from the Spirit. There is discernment between the voice of his Master and the leading of the flesh. "And when he putteth forth his own sheep, he goeth before them, and the sheep follow him: for they know his voice" (John 10:4). Do you have an ear for the voice of the Good Shepherd, and do you have experience in following Him?

"My husband works a full-time job plus has his own business. We are trying to get debt free. He would love to be home more, but until we pay off our debt that we have created, we have to make a huge sacrifice. It does make me sad though. The children and I miss seeing him as often as we would like to. Although we have scheduled a 'family Bible time' for each Sunday night, it somehow gets missed for other things. At this point we all do our Bible reading and quiet time as individuals."

For a man to be called to a home business, I would expect to see him be debt free or seriously working toward it without impacting his family time. Just as the above comment indicates, debt causes a man to think he has to spend his time working rather than investing it in his family.

"The rich ruleth over the poor, and the borrower *is* servant to the lender" (Proverbs 22:7). "Owe no man any thing, but to love one another: for he that loveth another hath fulfilled the law" (Romans 13:8). The man who has no debt is not in bondage to another and is able to live on far less than someone with debt. He has proven he has self-control in finances, and he will need this discipline if he starts his own business.

"My husband is self-employed and works way too many hours. It is very frustrating to me. Our pastor preached this Sunday about committing to quit work at a certain time each day and leaving it in the Lord's hands. I am praying that God is working on my husband's heart to see that he is neglecting his family and his wife in trying to provide for us in his own strength. It has caused a wall between us that I don't think he sees. Only time will tell if it is repairable."

This is the reality of a home business—no quitting time and no days off work—unless one makes separating work and family time a priority and a conscious decision. Therefore, I would also expect to see a man who can manage his time. In a home business, there are many time pressures with no real constraints on when work time should end each day. If a dad hasn't put leading his family as the highest priority below the Lord when working for someone else, it will only get worse when he is the "boss." That dad has not proven himself, and he will struggle more with his time when he has his own business.

> The vast majority of people I know who own a small business don't "have" time for their families. Seeing that has deterred me from jumping on the "own your own business" bandwagon. There is a lot of pressure in "Christian" circles on both men and women, that godly men will own their own businesses. My wife mentioned that she felt guilty for years that we didn't own a business.

"My husband owns his own business so he works an insane amount of hours."

I hear of dads who are drowning in their home businesses and sadly then turn to their wives to solve the problem. A dad will begin heaping work on his wife, and a bad situation gets worse. Then the natural progression, if the family is homeschooling, is to put their children in school because Mom's time is now diverted from the children to the business. However, I question whether God's solution for keeping a business afloat is going to involve risking the negative consequences of moving children from a homeschool environment to a school.

I would expect to see a man who would hear a calling to a particular business only if that business was consistent with Scripture and his vision. Consider a pawn shop, for example. It usually profits on others' hardships and can involve the sale of unwholesome merchandise. Would the Lord be calling a dad to that business?

Christopher, our second born, has a gift for photography. He began "shooting" Christian weddings when he was twenty. However, it didn't take long to realize that this was not a wholesome business due to the immodesty in the bridal parties. He stopped accepting weddings for a period of time until he realized he could have some criteria to screen for those weddings he could accept. If a business is God's calling, it will neither be a stumbling block to the "customers" nor to the one engaged in the business. God's calling will bring glory to God. "Whether therefore ye eat, or drink, or whatsoever ye do, do all to the glory of God" (1 Corinthians 10:31).

Finally, I would expect to see a man who isn't afraid of problems. When you are an employee, you can take your problems to your boss. Ultimately, every problem is his problem. But when you are the boss, all problems come to you. If a dad doesn't manage the family problems well, doesn't want to hear about them, and won't resolve them, then I am confident God is not calling this man to a home business unless it is to chasten him. From what I have observed, a home business is a great paddle when in the hand of the Lord and applied to a wayward dad. If you are handling your current problems well, God may be calling you to a home business.

> I've also seen a man's choice of business pull his wife away from homeschooling and be a temptation. She now sees it as her business, and she is involved in managing it, reverses roles, or at least reduces or eliminates her mother role, and gives two providers. Thanks for sharing the negatives of owning a business.

Will It Build Up the Family?

Is a man committed to building up the family through his home business and avoiding what tears it down? A home business can bring stress to a family, or it can bring blessings.

In 1997 when the Lord clearly took me out of my corporate job as an engineer, I came home to work in Communication Concepts. Christopher had just graduated from high school. At that point, we felt the Lord's direction that he, Nathan (my oldest), and I would work together in Communication Concepts, which we had established when Nathan graduated from high school two years earlier. Nathan performed computer work for Kansas City area businesses, but Christopher and I would broker printing. Working with my boys was a fulfillment of the vision the Lord had put on my heart years earlier. Even though I spent many days making sales calls alone, I loved being with my family more.

Our home business allowed me to teach my sons business skills, help them grow in their ability to rely on the Lord for direction and peace, and manage their time. I was also able to begin incorporating some of the younger children in our business as well.

In time we had some large projects that consisted of compiling and assembling three-ring notebooks with contents and tabs. This was something the older school-age children could do. We found we greatly enjoyed working together. It was also a blessing for those children who were old enough to be involved in the project because they were paid as independent contractors, which helped their savings accounts.

We have been able to avoid having others work for us since I let my children have responsibilities in our business when they are capable. I am training them, they are learning skills, and we are working together as a family in a sheltered environment. As each graduates from high school, they have been able to join us in our Communications Concepts work, help in the ministry work, or branch out by starting a new business. Everyone wins.

I have a couple of words of caution, though. If you consider involving your children in a home business, there are child labor laws that have to be evaluated. Each dad contemplating having his children working with him must be satisfied that he is abiding by the law.

In addition, we have known some who use their children in a home business but don't pay them for their help. Yes, the children do receive blessings from the business simply from being a part of the family, but the Lord has an eye on the laborer who does not receive fair wages. "Woe unto him that buildeth his house by unrighteousness, and his chambers by wrong; *that* useth his neighbour's service without wages, and giveth him not for his work" (Jeremiah 22:13). I would never want to take advantage of my children's help, nor cause my Lord to be displeased, so we have always paid the children a very fair wage.

God Requires Us to Work

Wouldn't it have been nice if the Lord had designed things so we didn't have to work? He could have made it so we didn't need to eat, or He could have provided manna just like He did for the Israelites. However, He said, "Six days shalt thou labour, and do all thy work" (Exodus 20:9). He also put the responsibility of discipling children on the father's back. "And, ye fathers, provoke not your children to wrath: but bring them up in the nurture and admonition of the Lord" (Ephesians 6:4). It may seem easier to provide a living that enables Mom to be home taking care of the children than it is to invest our off-work hours raising children to be dynamic followers of the Lord Jesus. May we be committed to our vital priority. We must be efficient with every minute we have, both at work and when we are home so that we can be redeeming our time.

Time for Sleep

Next to work, sleep is our biggest time block for each day, so it is important that we manage it well. Sleep is an amazing thing. It is bittersweet in that it is pleasurable and necessary, but for every hour we sleep, we are unable to use that time for something else. I have to admit I have occasionally coveted those seven-plus hours of sleep to be used for other endeavors. Life would have been much simpler without the necessity of sleep, and certainly more productive. However, sleep is part of God's plan, and we work within God's design, considering the capabilities of the body. Therefore, we obviously need to sleep every day.

God's Plan

As we look at how sleep affects our time-management process, we want to understand the Lord's view on sleep for His servants. Sometimes as we study the Word, we find that His outlook on something is different from ours. If we live contrary to His plan for us, we can expect frustration and a lack of blessing. So if we are to learn how to manage our sleep time, we should review what Scripture tells us about sleep.

When we go through all the verses that refer to sleep in some way, we don't see any that exhort believers to get enough sleep. As necessary as we know sleep is, why didn't the Lord encourage His servants to be well rested? Why didn't He tell them to make sure they were getting enough sleep? Let's take a brief look at some verses in Proverbs for the answer.

> "How long wilt thou sleep, O sluggard? when wilt thou arise out of thy sleep?" (Proverbs 6:9). Here the lazy person is associated with too much sleep.

> "He that gathereth in summer *is* a wise son: *but* he that sleepeth in harvest *is* a son that causeth shame" (Proverbs 10:5). The person who causes shame is sleeping when he should be working.

> "Slothfulness casteth into a deep sleep; and an idle soul shall suffer hunger" (Proverbs 19:15). Laziness promotes sleep.

> "Love not sleep, lest thou come to poverty; open thine eyes, *and* thou shalt be satisfied with bread" (Proverbs 20:13). Loving sleep will bring a man to poverty.

I find sleep as pleasant as anyone else, but the Bible tells me it is associated with someone lazy, and it will lead to poverty. Since God owns my time, I must see getting too much sleep as something to be guarded against. The flesh tends toward being lazy and will want more sleep than it really needs. Therefore we understand that God didn't exhort us to get enough sleep, because the body is self-regulating. It has a way of communicating with us if we are falling too far behind in our sleep. It becomes clear, from the warnings of Scripture, that it is better to err on the side of too little sleep than too much. "Six days shalt thou labour, and do all thy work" (Exodus 20:9). Since we are told to work six days, my choice is to "push hard" getting a minimum amount of sleep for six days and then have a day of rest.

In order to manage my sleep time, having a biblical perspective of sleep is an important starting point. When I view sleep as God views it, I can manage those hours of my day in obedience to Him and His Word. I can shun following the flesh and delight in self-denial, looking for the blessings that accompany this choice.

The Blessing of Rising Early

There is something about getting up early that divides the men from the boys. Real men rise up early. Are we early risers? Look at the partial list of examples of rising early:

> Abraham rose early when sending Hagar away. Genesis 21:14

> Abraham rose early to go sacrifice Isaac. Genesis 22:3

> Jacob rose early to build an altar. Genesis 28:18

> Moses rose early to build an altar. Exodus 24:4

> Moses rose early to go back up Mount Sinai. Exodus 34:4

> Joshua led the nation and rose early to enter the promised land. Joshua 3:1

> Joshua with the nation rose early and circled Jericho. Joshua 6:12

> Joshua with the nation rose early and took Jericho. Joshua 6:15

> Joshua with the nation rose early to find Achan's sin. Joshua 7:16

> Joshua with the nation rose early to take Ai. Joshua 8:10

> Gideon rose early to check the fleece. Judges 6:38

> Gideon rose early to select his soldiers. Judges 7:1

David rose early on the day he fought Goliath. 1 Samuel 17:20

David and his men rose early to leave Achish. 1 Samuel 29:11

Absalom rose early to steal the hearts of the people. 2 Samuel 15:2

God rose early to speak. Jeremiah 7:13, 25:3, 35:14

God rose early daily to send His prophets. Jeremiah 7:25, 25:4, 26:5, 29:19, 35:15, 44:4

God rose early to tell His people to obey. Jeremiah 11:7

God rose early to teach. Jeremiah 32:33

Jesus rose early to pray. Mark 1:35, Luke 21:38

Jesus rose early to teach. John 8:2

Jesus rose early to meet the disciples, who had been fishing all night. John 21:4

Are we just as likely to get up early to paint the house as we are when we are leaving on vacation? There is a mixture of both pleasant and unpleasant tasks in life, and we should have the mindset that we get up early to do what must be done no matter what it is. Abraham rose early to go to sacrifice Isaac and to send Ishmael and Hagar away, both of which would have been difficult to do.

There is great benefit when we get up early at the same time every morning, regardless of whether it is a working day. Almost everyone has heard Benjamin Franklin's quote, "Early to bed and early to rise makes a man healthy, wealthy and wise." God didn't promise wealth by getting up early, but He did promise poverty if we like to sleep too much. "*Yet* a little sleep, a little slumber, a little folding of the hands to sleep: So shall thy poverty come as one that travelleth, and thy want as an armed man" (Proverbs 6:10-11). We will be a blessing to our children and their children as we learn to number our days. Rising early is a key part of that.

"My husband is self-employed and works very hard to get ahead. He does best when he rises early to work."

I commend this dad for getting up early to work, even though he is self-employed and could sleep later. Dads often awake early during the week to make it to work, but there are also blessings for the diligent man who will rise early every day. This is a great starting place for time management.

I want to slip in a blessing I've experienced in the mornings due to my daily schedule and learning more about the importance of rising early. One of my greatest struggles is finding time to memorize Scripture. I used to memorize consistently when I commuted, but since my office is now in my home, I have struggled with memory time. Recently I revised my morning schedule, setting the alarm clock for ten minutes earlier than it had previously been set. I now wake up at 5:10 and am dressed and ready to leave the bedroom by 5:30. I then go to my desk and spend that extra ten minutes memorizing Scripture. I haven't missed those ten minutes of sleep either. Making Scripture memory a part of my daily schedule allows me to work on my verses before I meet the children in the living room for our individual Bible reading at 5:45 a.m. What a joy and blessing that has been. "O God, thou *art* my God; early will I seek thee: my soul thirsteth for thee, my flesh longeth for thee in a dry and thirsty land, where no water is" (Psalms 63:1).

The Right Amount of Sleep

Scripture does not give us a formula for finding the correct amount of sleep, nor does it specify how much sleep we should have. It just cautions about getting too much sleep. It would be nice if the Lord gave us explicit directions on the right amount of sleep, but as with food, we must determine for ourselves how much our body needs to sustain normal life. It will take experimentation and the willingness to be a little tired to come up with that total. However, once the target amount of sleep is "dialed in," life is quite sustainable even though some days one may be slightly more tired than others.

I have found that eight hours of sleep a night is wonderful. However, if I get seven and a half to seven hours and fifteen minutes, I manage quite well even though I'm just a little tired. I can consistently get along with seven hours of sleep a night, but I am more tired during the day than I prefer. If I'm at my desk very long, I will have trouble staying awake. When we are on the road, I will get about seven hours of sleep at night, but I can make up for that by a short nap before conferences while the children set up.

To find out how much sleep you really need, it will take some experimentation. Because the demands of each day can vary, have a two- or three-week trial period. You probably have at least some idea how much sleep you need, so you can begin by picking fifteen minutes less a night. Select a wakeup time in the morning that will allow you to have at least twenty minutes reading your Bible and ten or fifteen minutes praying. The more time in the Word the better, but try that amount first if you aren't currently having a devotion in the morning.

I have found that life changes frequently, and sometimes we don't receive the amount of sleep each night we would like to get. Even though we no longer have babies in our home, there are other interruptions that come in the middle of the night. A great example is that, since we live in Kansas, it is common to have a thunderstorm roll through during spring and summer months. We have a dog who is terrified of storms and sleeps in our room. She wakes up as soon as she hears distant thunder, and she shakes and whines until the storm is long gone. She is loud enough to wake Teri and me up even though we wear foam earplugs. However, I can still get up the next morning at my designated wakeup time and make it fine through the day on those occasions.

After a few weeks of experimentation to find the least amount of sleep you need, discuss with your wife how she thinks you have done and compare that against your own assessment. Have you found the right amount, where you are rested but maybe just a little tired during the day? If you are too tired, then add fifteen minutes a night and try that for a couple of weeks. If you are getting too much sleep, is it possible to cut back another fifteen to thirty minutes? If there have been a lot of interruptions in the nights, such as from a sick child, then it might be good to continue the experiment for another few weeks so a reasonable evaluation can be made. But once you know the amount, you can work at making it consistent.

"My hubby works from home several days a week, and on those days he obviously has no commute. On days he goes to the office, he has an hour commute each way, so that cuts an hour off his sleep time in the AM."

Here is a man who has found he can get by with less sleep on the days he has a commute to work because he is able to sleep a normal number of hours on the days he works from home. Another option for him would be to go to sleep earlier every night, allowing for the amount of sleep he really needs on commute days. Then he could get up consistently at the same time every morning, begin work earlier on his work-from-home days, and be ready for an earlier bedtime.

Bedtimes Are Critical to Managing Your Time

Years ago I found that if I set my alarm clock each night to get a certain amount of sleep based on the time I went to bed, I wouldn't feel as rested as when I went to sleep and woke up at the same time every day. I have read a couple of sleep study summaries, and they have affirmed that a consistent bedtime is very helpful in getting a good night's sleep. The body is wonderfully made, and if we go to bed at the same time, it will begin shutting down in preparation for sleep. I prefer to be able to turn the light out and quickly fall to sleep versus lying in bed for a half hour or so trying to go to sleep.

When I am getting a reasonable amount of sleep each night, it is much easier to get up and have my time in the Word. For over twenty years, I've been blessed to have a daily time reading my Bible in the morning. There have been some mornings that I was very tired, and I had to work to stay awake, but that isn't the norm. I love my time in the Word, and being awake to savor each minute of it is very important to me. Therefore, I make every effort to be in bed at the time I have set. After all of these years, I have no regrets over rising up early enough to spend time in the Word every morning, but I have experienced innumerable blessings as a result.

"My husband counts his hour and fifteen minute commute to work as his quiet time, though he believes he should do it before he leaves. (He's always too tired to get up and do that.)"

I agree that a man should have his personal time in the Word before he leaves for work. Especially with a long commute, it is tempting to try to use that time to listen to the Bible on a CD or MP3 player and pray, calling that our time in the Word. However, I know from personal experience that it just isn't the same as reading a Bible in the privacy of our homes where there isn't the constant distraction of traffic and scenery. Be determined to go to bed early enough that you can get up in the morning for time in the Word before you leave for work. Set the alarm clock and make yourself get up whether you feel like it or not. A shower before Bible reading will help wake you up if you are struggling with that.

I have found it is important to be disciplined to head for bed at least thirty minutes prior to when I want to go to sleep. Every night at 9:15, I shut down my computer. I then "make my rounds" by locking up the house, turning off lights, checking the thermostat, and turning on the security alarm. As I continue this process, I might notice a piece of mail or a bill on the counter that grabs my attention. The temptation is to deal with it then, but that is how I get sidetracked and miss being in bed on time. I will bring it with me and put it on the bathroom vanity to be dealt with in the morning. It takes great care not to be deterred from being in bed on time.

Once I've finished my "rounds," I brush my teeth, read Teri a chapter from the New Testament, turn the lights off, and then pray with her. Teri and I have a "race" to see who is asleep first. I almost always win and am asleep within a minute or two because I am very ready for sleep. Teri, on the other hand, doesn't need as much sleep as I do, so it will take her a little while to fall asleep. I'm convinced I fall asleep so quickly because I err on the side of just a bit too little sleep and maintain the same bedtime every night.

Other Important Factors

There are some other important factors that can greatly affect the sleep equation. If we ignore them, we will struggle with managing our sleep time and be frustrated. There are many challenges that a dad faces each day, and it is important to nail down those that can be managed. There will always be things beyond your control, but the more we can regulate, the less impact other factors will have.

I'm assuming that most men reading this book are married; therefore, the sleep needs of your wife should be considered. Obviously, she may require more or less sleep than you do. How well has your wife done with the same quantity of sleep you have received during the experimentation time? Is she waking up to nurse a baby or care for a little one? Are there other factors that might affect how much sleep she needs?

After Nathan, our first child, was born, we discovered that sleep and babies were a difficult combination. Sleep deprivation can have great negative impact on a person's cheerful countenance, even to the point of depression. We began looking for ways to make sure Teri was able to sleep.

There were times when she needed to sleep later in the morning after being up nursing in the night. We have always gone to bed together, but I would slip out of bed before her in the morning during those seasons so she could get additional sleep. She might also take naps when the baby was sleeping during the day.

Years later when Teri was still having babies and had developed even more difficulties with sleeping, the Lord led us to having her try foam earplugs. They worked well, and in fact, she still uses them twenty years later. So that she could sleep, I then became the ears at night and would wake her up if need be. The earplugs have helped Teri sleep even though we no longer have little ones because I have become an off-and-on snorer.

Teri now is the one who needs less sleep than I do. So, when she wakes up early, she is content to lie quietly praying and going over memory verses in her mind until the alarm sounds. Through the years, we have managed to adjust the wakeup times to allow us to go to sleep together.

"We have six children and Daddy works sometimes 45-50 hours a week. We have a nursing baby who is awake often during the night so neither my husband nor I get consistent hours of sleep."

I encourage dads to work with their wives in helping to get babies to sleep through the night. With three nonscheduled babies and five scheduled babies, we found that our scheduled babies slept through the night much earlier than our nonscheduled babies. I can't begin to tell you the blessings to both Mom and the whole family when a baby is sleeping through the night, allowing Mom and Dad to have an uninterrupted night's sleep. Many moms are resistant to using a schedule with their babies because of the negative information about schedules presented by scheduling opponents. We have not experienced those negative outcomes, but rather we have been hugely benefitted and blessed by scheduling our babies. We have shared information about scheduling babies in our book *Managers of Their Homes* (see Resources at the back of the book), if you would have a need for this kind of help.

It's Worth the Effort

Sleep is usually the second biggest block of time in our schedule. Therefore, we want to be good stewards of our time and keep a close rein on the amount of sleep we receive. Scripture warns against getting too much sleep and details the outcomes for those who love sleep. Rising early is often found in Scripture and presented in a positive light. If we develop the habit of rising early in the morning, we will reap benefits in our quest for self-discipline and in our time management. Critical to gaining the most rest during our sleep hours is going to bed at a consistent time. It will take some determination to be successful. I can assure you that the effort is worth it, and that you will find yourself redeeming your time. A reasonable amount of sleep each night provides a solid foundation to managing all of our time in the way the Lord leads.

Time During the Week

The hours we have in our weekdays after work are valuable to us in our time management. It may seem that we don't have much time during the week available to us, but as we learn to redeem the time, these hours are very precious. Managed well, they allow us to accomplish much of what God has called us to do in spiritually leading our families and keeping up with the other responsibilities He has placed into our lives.

A Treadmill Existence?

Teri's dad had a treadmill in his basement that he ran on during bad weather. I used it a few times, and it was always a real burden to run on it. There was something about exerting myself, having sweat pouring down my face, and yet never getting anywhere that made the workout drudgery to me. I wonder if that isn't how many dads feel about their weekdays. They spend time at work and go home only to get up the next morning to have it all begin again, always under a feeling of pressure because they aren't keeping up.

On a recent survey regarding men's time, 82 percent of the households responding indicated that Dad was under time pressure. Jesus said, "Peace I leave with you, my peace I give unto you: not as the world giveth, give I unto you. Let not your heart be troubled, neither let it be afraid" (John 14:27). Then where is the peace?

I've known very few men who seemed to have enough time. There is always much more to do with our time than there is time to do it. We need to come to the point of seeing that it is okay to feel like we have more to do in a day than we have time for and be at peace knowing the Lord will never give us more than there is time to do. When we have limited amounts of something precious, we have to be good stewards of it to make it stretch. After finishing our vocational work each day, there isn't much left of the day. The question is, how faithful will we be with that

I always liken it to those guys who spin plates on the thin wooden dowels. They'll have twenty of those going and are frantically running around trying to keep them all spinning.

precious amount of time? If we are using our time as the Lord directs, then it is a conscious decision to be at peace knowing the Lord will direct our priorities as is pleasing to Him.

I remember when we were living in Clearwater, Florida. I had left an engineering job and was working for a small computer store selling dedicated computer estimating systems to general, electric, and plumbing contractors. My income was strictly based on sales commissions, and if it wasn't for the Lord, we would have starved. Money was scarce during the year that I worked there because I only sold a few systems. We had to be extremely frugal with what little money we had. In the same way, we must be ultra careful with the limited amount of time that we have in order to make it stretch as far as it possibly can.

Little by Little

When we came to Kansas City, I was working for a company that produced aircraft landing and navigation systems, and I commuted around fifty minutes each way. I bought an old Toyota Tercel for $1,600 that needed work. We replaced many parts on the car, and it ran fairly well for four years. However, the mileage was adding up, and it was beginning to show its age. Without reliable transportation, I would have a problem soon, but we didn't have the money to buy another car. We were committed not to borrow, but what can you do if you need a car and don't have the money?

At that point of time, Teri was stronger than I was in not borrowing, and she was a wonderful helpmeet in encouraging that we trust the Lord to keep the Toyota running while we saved everything we could toward the purchase of another car. Even though it looked rather futile, we began praying and saving every possible penny. God so blessed those efforts, and in time, before the car broke down, we had over ten thousand dollars—enough to trade in that Tercel and buy a Honda Civic with cash! What excitement I had to see how God took what little we could save each week and multiplied it.

Just after that, we developed some leaks in our roof over the garage. It was clear we needed a new roof, but again, we didn't have the money. We decided to begin saving every bit we could toward a new roof. In the meantime, I bought a gallon of "blackjack" roof repair and smeared it all over the troublesome valleys. In a little over a year's time, we were able to buy a new roof and have it installed. As we achieve victories over the use of "little," there is a growing motivation that spurs us on.

Is our attitude one of needing to be ever so careful with the limited amount of time we have each evening? The flesh cries out that it deserves to relax after a hard day's work. Let me ask you a couple questions. What about your wife? Has she worked hard all day? Does she deserve to take it easy all evening? Some might think, "Wait a minute. If my wife relaxes all night, who is going to fix dinner, clean up the mess, and then put the children to bed?"

The reality is, neither Dad nor Mom have the luxury of being able spend their evenings just relaxing. Let's look at a section of Scripture that helps us gain a biblical perspective on our usage of our evening hours.

> "But which of you, having a servant plowing or feeding cattle, will say unto him by and by, when he is come from the field, Go and sit down to meat? And will not rather say unto him, Make ready wherewith I may sup, and gird thyself, and serve me, till I have eaten and drunken; and afterward thou shalt eat and drink? Doth he thank that servant because he did the things that were commanded him? I trow not. So likewise ye, when ye shall have done all those things which are commanded you, say, We are unprofitable servants: we have done that which was our duty to do" (Luke 17:7-10).

These verses show us what the Lord expects of us, and how different His opinion is of how we use our time from what our flesh craves. The days are short, and eternity will be upon us before we realize it. We must "make hay while the sun shines" and not let little bits of time slip through our hands. We should redeem the time and learn to number our days little by little.

What It Adds Up to Be

Let's assume the average dad works forty hours a week and has an hour daily commute. It takes him fifteen minutes at the beginning and end of work to get from the parking lot to his desk or vice versa, and he has an hour for lunch. That means he is away from home ten and a half hours a day.

If he gets up at 5:30 a.m., spends a half hour getting ready for work, has forty-five minutes of Bible time and prayer, and grabs a quick fifteen-minute breakfast, he would leave for work at seven. He will be back home at 5:30 p.m. Dinner can be at 6:00 and all cleaned up by 7:00 at the latest. Based on the amount of sleep men reported they needed in the survey, most men will have three or four hours an evening available for something profitable.

If a man is careful with his time, that represents between fifteen and twenty discretionary hours during the weeknights, sixty to eighty hours a month, 780 to 1,040 hours a year and 15,600 to 20,800 hours over twenty years. What we view as so little can be seen to represent a great deal of time. Think about how important those 20,000 hours are in shaping the lives of our children.

We could take an extreme example of a dad who has a crazy schedule. Let's say he had only two hours at home a night with the family during the week. Taking thirty minutes to eat, thirty minutes to get ready for bed, he would be left with only sixty minutes of discretionary time a night, which adds up to five a week, twenty a month, 260 a year and 5,200 hours over twenty years. What if that dad felt that he had worked hard and deserved an hour of TV in the evening? At the end of twenty years, he would have had zero weekday time with his children. How could a dad ever face the Lord Jesus and give an accounting for such time usage?

We have a very limited amount of time each weekday to bring up our children in the nurture and admonition of the Lord. The less discretionary time we have, the greater our dedication must be not to waste a minute. Whether we have zero, one, five, or ten children, our time is precious, and the Lord has a purpose for how it is to be used. Instead of thinking of our discretionary time in hour increments, it would be better to think in minutes. Every dad must view each minute as precious, but for the dad who has so little time with his family, he has to consider every minute to be priceless. Once we come to the place of realizing that we can't afford to squander our weekday time, we are ready to look at how we can use it.

Looking for Bargains

The nursery where I buy fertilizer for the yard has a promotion of which I take advantage. Through the year, they give you a "value buck" for every ten dollars you spend with them. Then during one week of the year, you can use your "value bucks." For every real dollar you pay, you can also cash in one "value buck." It is the same as giving you a net 5 percent discount on your total purchases for the year, but it seems more like a 50 percent discount the way they work it. I want to "cash in" on those savings. In a similar way, I desire to be a good steward of my time so that for every minute I "spend," I am getting all the value I can possibly get for it. This is part of redeeming the time.

Earning a living will eat up much of our day, so we have to guard the crumbs of time that are left over. Teri is a master when it comes to using leftovers. She can stretch our food budget amazingly far by a careful use of leftovers. It is like value bucks for our food budget. In the same way, we can take our leftover pieces of time and accomplish tasks little by little and not twiddle it away. As we do more with time that was previously lost, we can turn a pressure-packed day into one that is still busy, but efficient and peaceful. We have peace when we are accomplishing all the Lord is calling us to because we know we are doing what He wants us to do.

Bible Time and Children's Bedtime

The most priceless use of time each day is that time when Dad leads his family reading and discussing the Bible. There is no greater value that can be received for our time. Think about it: we have the opportunity to influence where a child will be for eternity and the quality of his life on earth. How could we spend time more profitably than that? Carving out and prioritizing time to lead our families in the Word every night needs to be at the top of the list. When we are in the Word every day, it is foundational to being at peace in the Lord. Don't expect peace if this isn't happening, but you can expect temptations to let other things take the place of what is most important.

For years I have put our boys to bed. It is a wonderful time because it draws our hearts together. There are always more things to share than there are minutes to talk. It is a very special time of fellowshipping first with each other and then with our Lord as we pray. It gives me the added blessing of being able to hear the things that are on my sons' hearts, with which they petition the Lord of glory. That allows me a look into their hearts and the chance to discuss important topics with them later—maybe during our Sunday meeting time. Putting the boys to bed in their younger years was also a benefit to Teri because if I hadn't done it, she would have, so it saved her time.

We must be on guard against getting off track with our time usage. There was recently an extended time when I lost sight of the important and gave in to the urgent. My list of things to be done is always a very long list, and I can take my eyes off of Jesus and look at those "waves" about me. If I do so, in essence, I'm choosing pressure over peace with Jesus.

> Every 2 months we review our time to see whether we are spending time on urgent or important issues. We often ask each other and ourselves, "Is this important, or urgent?"

At one point, I took my eyes off of the priority of putting my sons to bed because I thought they were certainly old enough at fourteen, eighteen, and twenty to go to bed by themselves—and of course, they were. I had plenty on which I could spend that half hour a night. However, before long the Lord put it on my heart to begin praying with them again at bedtime, and it opened my eyes to the fact that I had deceived myself. We have such a blessed time of talking and then praying. I can't believe I put other things ahead of that important time. Had I looked to my vision statement, I wouldn't have dropped the time in the first place, because our prayer and fellowship leads to the development in my sons of many of the aspects in that vision statement. I desire to spend every minute of my day the way the Lord would have me to, and I can see that relationships need to be high on the list.

Errands

I am always open to errands that can be run with the children on weekday evenings in the time available around dinner, family Bible time, and bedtime. I may take multiple children with me or just one child so I can have one-on-one time with him. Have you ever lacked for things to talk about with a child? If so, it is likely because you haven't cultivated a relationship with him. It takes time to be able to communicate on a deeper level with anyone, and most certainly that would be true of a child. Errands are good opportunities because while you are out together, you will see and experience a host of things that are springboards for discussion. Errands are powerful value bucks in the hand of a skillful father building relationships with his family.

For almost twenty years, I did all the grocery shopping on a weeknight with the children. It took an hour or a little less, and we all looked forward to it. I would have a baby in a backpack, another child in the cart seat, and the others alongside us. As the children got older, we would "attack" the grocery store in force. The children would spread out by pairs getting an item or two on the list, returning to be sent out again. We would laugh and have a wonderful time together. At the check out, each child always got to pick out a candy bar to eat, and we would buy the cashier one as well.

Another blessing of me taking the children on errands was that Teri had some time to herself. Sometimes she would catch up on things she needed to do, but while we were out buying groceries, her "standing order" was to enjoy the quiet and take a bath. It was an hour that she spent reading, thinking, and praying. Our grocery time paid value-buck dividends in Teri's life as well.

OJT

In the Air Force, we referred to the way we learned as On the Job Training (OJT), and we have carried on that tradition strongly in our family without calling it by that name. Whenever there is OJT going on, there are value bucks. I'm having fellowship with the one learning, he is gaining a skill, and there is the added blessing of equipping him to be able to help others with what he is learning. Now *that* is value-buck multiplication of time!

One of the best OJT examples is running errands together. The children are able to watch my interactions with those with whom we come into contact. I will speak with store clerks and other customers. If the person is a Christian, the Lord would have me encourage him in his walk. If he is lost, then I want to share Christ with him. Often there is only time for partial sharing, but I know the Lord will send someone else along to tell more of the story. Not only is the Lord able to use me in situations like that, but He is allowing the children to observe and learn. They see how easy it is and how most people aren't offended but grateful for what I share. Through this process my children learn conversation skills, and later they may transition to more in-depth spiritual discussions with others. This is an example of the value-buck principle applied to time. I spend my time grocery shopping, and the value-buck benefit is the fellowship I have with my children, the quiet Teri enjoys, and the opportunity to teach my children how to witness.

Exercise Profiteth Little

Ever since 1977, I have exercised most days, except Sundays, unless I had some sort of injury. There was a long "season" where the time I spent exercising was excessive and frankly a waste of time. For a number of years, I was running over forty miles a week, and there were times when it was over sixty miles. Considering my pace, that was a lot of time, and for what real purpose? "For bodily exercise profiteth little: but godliness is profitable unto all things, having promise of the life that now is, and of that which is to come" (1 Timothy 4:8). Even if it was an enjoyable use of time, compared to spending the time with my children, I could never justify it before the Lord. The body is the temple of the Holy Spirit, and we are to take care of it, but studies I have read indicate that good health can be attained in far less time than I was investing.

Through the years, I've met many who waste great amounts of time in the name of "exercise." For example, I've known some people who have chosen to go to gyms to exercise. Considering it takes ten to fifteen minutes to travel somewhere, an hour for a typical workout, and thirty minutes to cool down and shower, such exercise can eat up to two hours of precious evening time. May we count the cost. If we were going to the gym just three evenings a week, that represents 312 hours a year. That doesn't take into consideration the worldly music that is usually blasting away, and if it is a co-ed facility, the defrauding "undress" that the women will be wearing. What a pit of temptation, affording great opportunity for a man's heart to stumble! Many a fallen man thought it could never happen to him, but it did. How much better to simply avoid the place and redeem time in the process. May we use our time as the Lord directs.

If we value our time there may be far better ways to exercise, and we can spend value bucks in the meantime. For over twenty years now, I include a family member with me when I exercise. For a period of time, I ran with Christopher in the morning before I left for work. After injuring my knee to the point that I could no longer run, I switched to walking with Teri's dad because Teri was already committed to walking with her mom. We fellowshipped as we walked. Over time we transitioned to where I walked with Teri, and her folks walked together. I'm guessing it has been over ten years now that Teri and I have walked together. During that time, there were some periods where an injury or the house-building project kept us from walking, but the norm is that we walk together. Teri and I get exercise while we discuss family, ministry, our relationship, and a multitude of other topics. Talk about value bucks at work!

Who Says You Can't Teach an Old Dog?

For years we structured our weeknights based on priorities, and we have gotten much accomplished. I had resisted following a schedule because I felt the demands for our time were too fluid to be confined by a schedule. I found out I was wrong.

Our schedule is pretty simple and roughly resembles what we had been doing for years. After work, we eat at 5:30, at 6:00 I do e-mail, at 6:30 we have family Bible time, at 7:30 we have family music practice, at 8:30 I work at my desk, at 8:45 I talk and pray with the boys, and at 9:15 I go back to my computer until 9:30, and then make my rounds, heading for bed.

Here are the benefits I have experienced over nonscheduled evenings.

> 1. I'm not asked every night about the exact time for our evening activities because everyone knows the schedule and is accountable for being ready to participate.

2. I don't have to track people down because they know when to be there.

3. Having an hour for family Bible allows us time to talk and time for a good devotion, plus an ending point.

4. The boys are ready for me to pray with them.

5. I'm consistently getting my desk work done because there is a time slot carved out for it.

About once a week or so, I will decide to cancel music practice to allow me to run a local errand, such as going to Home Depot for some supplies for a project. I will skip music practice and my desk time, but I want to be home by nine to put my boys to bed. That is a priority with my time—directed by my vision statement. As I evaluate our current needs while remaining faithful to our evening schedule, I have the flexibility to change it once in a while for a specific situation.

Just Fifteen Minutes

What do you wish to accomplish, but simply cannot find a place for it in your time management plan? Maybe you want time to talk to your children individually. Try applying a fifteen-minute rule. Carve fifteen minutes out of your evening, and spend it with one of your children one evening and another the next.

What about learning to play an instrument? Practice it for just fifteen minutes each night. Maybe you want to have time to research a home-repair project on the Internet. Do it with a fifteen-minute computer time slot, and be faithful to remain on the computer only for the allotted amount of time.

Life with Little Children

As the comments in this section indicate, life with young children bring a time pressure and need for time management that is in a category by itself. I want you to read about these families' struggles, and then how I believe time-management strategies will help them.

"We have five children, ages three to twelve, and that is where the time 'pressure' comes in. The younger ones still need so much care, training, and supervision, and we both feel stretched to the limit since we are homeschooling four of them. We wish to have more time to invest in them spiritually and educationally and then personally, as well, and feel like we don't have the time we need."

A homeschooling family has ample time to give to their children both spiritually and educationally. That is one of the greatest blessings of homeschooling. Since lack of time is a problem for this family, I would suggest that Dad help Mom set up a schedule for herself and the children during the day. Our book *Managers of Their Homes* is a tool you can use if you want assistance with this process. Then, with the combination of Dad's evening schedule and Mom's daytime schedule, I believe this family will remove the time pressure and meet the goals they have for their family.

"My husband says he struggles with balancing work and family time. We have all 'littles' right now, so that in itself is time consuming. He would like to cut down overtime at work but doesn't feel like he can."

Here again, I want to push you to use a schedule. Until you actually try it, you can have no concept of how much more productive and efficient your time will become. What was impossible becomes achievable. When overtime is optional, I suggest a dad put his family time as a higher priority than overtime. Rest in the Lord, and see how He will provide for the needs of the family. So often in these cases, we are fearful to make the decision for family because of the impact we think it will have to our finances or our job security. In reality it comes down to the fact that we are trusting in ourselves to provide rather than trusting in our Lord Jesus.

"My husband struggles with keeping a balance between accomplishing home tasks and spending quality time with the children. For instance, he must do work in the garden, but he also feels a pull to spend that short period of time with the children."

This is an excellent example for us to use. If we incorporate our children in our home tasks, we will be using those value bucks, because we can accomplish our work while spending time with one or more of the children. I would suggest that this dad have gardening in his schedule every evening after dinner. Split the children between Mom for the cleanup team and Dad for the gardening team. If there is a baby involved, put him in the backpack. Give the toddler a weed-pulling area where he isn't going to ruin a good plant. Have everyone working close enough together that all of you can talk.

Here is what is happening. The gardening is being done. Dad is fellowshipping with his children. The children are becoming diligent workers, and they are learning gardening skills in the process. Time is not being wasted in front of the TV or on computer games. That is value bucks at work.

"We would love to have family devotions on a more regular basis as well. Our children are an eleven-month-old girl, four-, five-, and seven-year-old boys, and eleven- and twelve-year-old girls. We always feel so fried and exhausted by the end of the day, and it's all we can do to get the children to bed!"

Again, I think that a schedule for the daytime hours for Mom and the children, combined with a schedule for the hours Dad is home, will alleviate the problem of being too tired to have family Bible time. Even if you are tired, I would encourage every dad to be committed to daily family Bible time. Be determined that the children don't go to bed until you have had Bible time with them. No matter how tired you feel, as the spiritual head of your home, being in the Word with your children is your vital priority—even more important than eating physical food.

"Most of my husband's time when he comes home is spent helping take care of the children with me until they go to bed, though he often finds a way to fit his computer games in."

Helping Mom with the children in the evening is positive. Since this note doesn't mention family time in the Word, I am assuming that isn't being done, so I suggest that change is facilitated. Perhaps ending the computer games will allow for Bible time.

Other Shifts

If you work a shift that is different from the traditional eight to five, this information still applies to you. You will simply translate evening hours to afternoon hours or morning hours, whatever the hours are that you have available that are not given to sleeping or working. I believe the importance of this information is even greater for you than it is for the man working normal business hours because it is easy for you not to be committed to accomplishing evening-type activities during other hours of the day. Sometimes we get in the mindset that Bible time happens in the evening or morning. "Since I am sleeping in the morning and working in the evening, I can't have Bible time with my family," is how the thinking goes. To begin productively using your open hours for family activities requires a change of thought.

When my family is on the road, we arrive at our conference location about 4:30, set up, eat dinner, and have our sessions. This means our evenings are full, and our nights are late.

Therefore, when we are traveling we have our family Bible time in the afternoons, normally around 3:30. A dad working second or swing shift will need to make similar adjustments to the family schedule. He might put family Bible time right after lunch followed by other family activities. This impacts your family's time and schedule. Work with your wife and help her learn to use the hours you are away at work for accomplishing the activities she would normally do in the early afternoon.

Dads who have a nontraditional schedule, such as having twenty-four hours on and then forty-eight hours off work, will benefit from applying what is in this chapter to the days they are home. With larger chunks of time at your disposal, you will be tempted to waste time if you don't have a plan and purpose for that time in mind before the day begins. You will likely be benefitted by working with your wife in how your days at home will be spent so that she can keep up with her home tasks. This is especially true if you are a homeschooling family. Find ways to facilitate the homeschooling when you are home rather than undermining it.

Too Precious to Waste

Totaling up each weeknight's hours helps us to understand what a significant block of time we have available to us. Since it comes in smaller quantities than our vocational or sleep time, it is very easy to let it slip through our fingers instead of being productive with it. Whether your vocational hours vary each day or are fixed, the evening time can be captured to be profitable if you are determined to use it. The clock is ticking, and eternity is one day closer each day. Are we learning to number our days? Are we redeeming our time? Is our time being used for God's glory according to His direction, or is the flesh winning on how we spend our time? The blessings are real, and the peace so sweet, if we will but yield to our Lord Jesus.

Days Off and Holidays

The next area of time management that we are going to tackle are days off work and holidays. These days will give us large chunks of time to be managed and allow us to accomplish what can't be done in the smaller snippets of time available before and after work.

I wonder if Saturdays, Sundays, and holidays are an unbeliever's idea of heaven on earth. At every corporate job I've had, it seemed like all the guys would talk about is what they were going to do on the weekend. For those who work a traditional schedule, Saturdays and holidays are the biggest single "chunk" of time we have available. The question is, how will we manage this time? How successful have we already been in making the most productive use of these gold mines of time? Are there ways we can be even better managers of our Saturdays and holidays?

What's Our Attitude?

Does our attitude mirror the world's when it comes to a day off? The worldly man wants to play and have fun when he is away from work. He feels that because he has worked hard all week, he deserves to relax and do what he wants to do. Are we lazy and entertainment minded? Are we lovers of pleasures more than lovers of God (2 Timothy 3:4)? What is our focus concerning our time usage when it is our time to manage?

I wonder if moms can look forward to Saturday as a day to have fun, kick back, and just relax all day. Personally, I doubt they have that luxury, because I think most moms are like Teri. She sees Saturday as a day to tackle the larger projects that she can't get to during the week. Do we deserve a "play day," but our wives don't?

The Lord said to us, "Six days shalt thou labour, and do all thy work" (Exodus 20:9). We men are supposed to be the stronger ones, right? "Likewise, ye husbands, dwell with *them* according to knowledge, giving honour unto the wife, as unto the weaker vessel, and as being heirs together of the grace of life; that your prayers be not hindered" (1 Peter 3:7). We are to set the example in the home of being the diligent, hardworking ones.

Look at this example from Scripture of what happens to us when we choose to give ourselves the break on Saturdays that we often think we deserve.

> "I went by the field of the slothful, and by the vineyard of the man void of understanding; And, lo, it was all grown over with thorns, *and* nettles had covered the face thereof, and the stone wall thereof was broken down. Then I saw, *and* considered *it* well: I looked upon *it, and* received instruction. *Yet* a little sleep, a little slumber, a little folding of the hands to sleep: So shall thy poverty come *as* one that travelleth; and thy want as an armed man" (Proverbs 24:30-34).

Are we hardworking or lazy? If someone walks by or visits in our home, what will they learn about us as they observe our home and yard maintenance? It is not a matter of how fancy, expensive, or decorated our homes are, but what we are doing with what the Lord has provided us.

I know times can be difficult, and money can be in short supply. It may be there is upkeep on the house needed without available money for the project. Are we being honest with ourselves? Perhaps the time and money had been there, but we used it for other pursuits such as entertainment, recreation, or hobbies. If a dad is in doubt as to whether he is being realistic in his evaluation of his time and money usage concerning home repairs, he can ask his wife, because she will likely have insight that he might be missing. Keeping the home in good repair is one way we can show our wives that we love them.

A man with an entertainment-oriented, lazy mindset will need to have very deep pockets if he wants to keep up with home responsibilities without doing the work himself. Most of us will have to make it a high priority in our schedules if we are going to keep our homes and lawns maintained, or we will fall behind. Even if someone has plenty of money to hire out the yard and home projects that must be done, he will miss out on the training and fellowship opportunities he might have had by including his children in his Saturday projects. Additionally, if he doesn't do these tasks, he will not be modeling diligence for his children.

"I, the wife, do the yard work. We pay to have the vehicle maintained, and we have many unfinished house duties."

This man pays for his car repairs, leaves the house repairs undone, and has a wife who is willing to undertake the yard work. How would his family relationships be built up by undertaking these jobs himself, maybe even working with his children? How would his finances be benefitted, and what could he teach his children in the process? I want to encourage you over and over concerning the blessing

> I have been surprised at how many men will not maintain their yards. They expect their wives to do it, along with caring for the house and family.

of choosing to be diligent and busy. We are so tempted to think we are tired, we need to rest, and we deserve a break. But I can tell you from personal experience, those attitudes only lead to negative results in a man's heart, in his family relationships, and in hindering his spiritual walk. The blessings and the joy come from being diligent and productive with our time, doing what we are called to do, and investing our time with our families.

Households responding to our survey reported that 65 percent of the dads were not satisfied with their ability to keep up with their home responsibilities. Without a detailed analysis of how each dad was spending his time, no one can know for sure, but it is likely that the time the Lord has given to take care of responsibilities is being used elsewhere. Perhaps some dads reading this book, who are feeling time pressure and not keeping up with their household tasks, might even question whether it is possible to get it all done. Please read the rest of the book with an open mind, and I can assure you, it is possible as long as we are following the Lord's direction for our time management. However, it will not be possible to fulfill the lusts of the flesh and the Lord's direction at the same time.

Our days off will test our resolve to be diligent, hardworking followers of the Lord Jesus. The temptation to go "play," as opposed to taking care of our responsibilities such as home, lawn, and vehicle maintenance, will be strongest on those days.

Practice What We, uh, Practice

We must keep in mind that far more important than bringing home a paycheck is bringing up our children in the nurture and admonition of the Lord. With the objective of raising men and women of God, we must not forget the power of our example. Our children are going to learn from our example much more quickly than they will from our words. Yes, preaching and teaching have a place, but our children are far more likely to follow how we live our lives than to follow empty words that we don't follow ourselves.

Here is an example of what happens when a man is serving God with his time, but not caring for the personal responsibilities the Lord has given to him.

"My husband works from home and is self-employed in the computer area. He spends much time at church in ministry and serving with his occupational knowledge, but spends zero time on any home responsibilities. He feels discipling and serving the Lord take precedence. I think that he needs to model responsibility at home for our children, so it's something that he still needs to figure out how to fit it in."

This man has a heart to serve the Lord with his time, but if he would learn to manage his time he could likely keep up with the maintenance of his home, lawn, and car. Not only will this be a blessing to his wife, but it will also be the example the children need to see in his life. Saturdays will most likely be the day he can utilize to allow time for home responsibilities and also his ministry.

The Key

I expect most of you have experienced Saturdays when you decided to sleep in until you felt like getting up. By the time you were dressed, showered, had time in the Word, and eaten breakfast, it was about time for lunch. The day was so far gone that it seemed like it had been wasted, and you didn't feel like tackling a big project because so much of the day was already past.

Back in the days of TV, I had this happen. Sleep in, eat larger breakfast, and watch football all day. What a waste that was. Now we work hard on Friday night and Saturday.

Eventually the day disappeared with nothing to show for those hours.

Do we sleep in on the weekends and holidays or delight in getting up early to see how much we can get done? Once again consider the impact that an hour here or there adds up to over the course of a month, a year, and ten years. If we choose not to sleep in two extra hours each Saturday, we gain over one hundred hours a year. That is the equivalent of one more week of productive life added on each year. What a blessing that would be.

The Secret Behind Brown Cow™

There is a type of yogurt in the health food stores in our area that I find to be delicious. I used to stop by a health food store when running errands during my lunch hour. I was hungry one day and decided to get some yogurt. Mmmmmmm. One of the reasons I found it so good is because there is a thin layer of cream on the top of the yogurt. That was the best yogurt I have ever tasted. The first bites are especially delightful. Just like that cream on the yogurt, getting up early and having our time in the Word and prayer every morning is the sweet, delicious way to begin our day, whether we are heading to work or having a day off.

This time in the Word and prayer will help us with our time management on days off and holidays just as it does during the work week, because we should have the Lord's direction for what we will do on these days too. Whatever projects we are tackling or however we are going to use those hours, it will be better when we have given it to the Lord in prayer as we start our day. Since projects are notorious for being problematic and going overtime, being in the Word is going to be a spiritually stabilizing force for dealing with those pressures.

Making the Best Use of the Day

I can't believe how creative my son, Joseph, is. He can design all sorts of things in his mind. However, we have discovered that just because something looks good in his mind, it doesn't mean it will always turn out that way. When we were building a house, there was a time or two when I heard these words from him: "I just don't know how that could have happened." The mental design had not transferred to something that worked when it was implemented. These experiences helped him see the value of putting things down on paper and how necessary that was to a successful project. It is easy to forget important details when they are only in one's mind.

Can you imagine preparing for a vacation, being all packed up, loading the car, and then realizing you hadn't decided where you were going? Most would say that is crazy, but isn't that similar to not knowing how you intend to spend a day off? In the past, I have wasted much time because Saturday morning arrived, and I didn't know what I was going to do. Sometimes I needed materials that I didn't have available, sometimes I needed the benefit of planning that hadn't been accomplished, sometimes I needed someone else to help who wasn't there, and sometimes I simply wasn't mentally prepared.

Maybe it is more pronounced with age, but I have found that there are projects that I have to be mentally prepared for before I can begin them. After we moved into the house we built, there were still a few things that needed to be done. One of them was painting the inside of the windows. It had been too cold earlier, so I was going to wait for several nice spring days after we moved in for the painting project. Then we could have all the windows out and paint without concern for rain or cold temperatures. However, once the first day came along that was acceptable, I hadn't mentally worked through all the necessary materials, where I would put the windows while I painted them, where they would dry, and how I would protect the area around where I was painting. Therefore, I lost the first day because of my lack of preparation, but I was ready the next good day.

On other days when I wasn't prepared, I found that my time began slipping through my fingers like sand, and then I would be frustrated. With only fifty-two Saturdays, seven national holidays, and then whatever number of vacation days we have, we can't afford to waste them. We are accountable to the Lord Jesus for how we use our time on earth. Time pressure comes from having things to do that require our time but not feeling we have enough time to accomplish them. Therefore, the key to being at peace is using our time efficiently under the Lord's direction. So let's look at how we can efficiently use our Saturdays and days off.

Dynamic and Specific

"Nothing becomes dynamic until it becomes specific." That was a common saying from our dear Pastor Anderson in Florida. He was encouraging his flock to be specific in what they were trying to accomplish.

We will save the details for a later chapter, but it will suffice for now to say that we must have a list of projects to do. As we become aware of needs, we put them on our list. Some projects will fit into the weekday evenings, and the rest can be accomplished on our days off.

What if a dad has no experience in home, lawn, or car maintenance? Does that mean he hires someone else to do these jobs? I would suggest that he learn how to do them himself. By doing this he will save the family money, he will gift his children because they will learn along with him, and he will gain new skills himself.

Just as you educate yourself for a task your boss gives you at work that you don't know how to do, educate yourself for your maintenance jobs. You can do this by reading books, doing Internet research, and talking to the experts. Start simple—practice makes perfect. As you master easier projects, work your way up to more complicated tasks. For example, changing the oil in your car is a pretty basic and routinely needed part of vehicle upkeep. On the Internet, you will find not only directions for how to change the oil but also videos demonstrating how to do it. This is true for most, if not all, areas of home, car, and lawn maintenance.

My oldest son, Nathan, grew up doing many household maintenance and building projects with me. Now that he has his own family, he continues the tradition of doing those jobs in his home. He often calls me for advice and suggestions for a project he is about to undertake, plus he has the Internet and a comprehensive home repair book for reference. Along with his successes, he has his share of stories that are familiar to anyone who does his own maintenance—stories of the project taking four times longer than expected and requiring multiple trips to the hardware store, of sweating in the attic in summer and freezing under a car in winter, of water spraying across the room from the pipe fitting that was turned the wrong way, and of needing to repaint a room because the color wasn't right. However, just like his dad, who faces those same kinds of problems, he keeps attempting his maintenance jobs and learning as he goes. May I encourage you to do the same?

If we learn to undertake listed items when we have the time for projects, such as on our days off, it will soon become automatic for us to go to the list rather than sit and do nothing. The more things we "move out of our minds" onto paper, the less pressure we will feel. When we no longer have to keep a "to do" list in our minds, it is like we have unloaded a backpack full of rocks that we had been carrying around with us all the time.

> I create a list for each Saturday, but it is always too long. I cross off what we finish and transfer the rest to next Saturday. I then put priorities on projects. (i.e. 15 on the list, but we work on top 8 first. If I finish those, I start working on others.) Also, we have a list in the laundry room for anyone to add on to or track progress. I add the activities to my list, and then I can prepare during the week.

For years moms have found this to be true when they have a schedule. They don't feel the pressure of all they have to do or what is next because it is scheduled. For us dads, we should have our list of things to do, tackling the highest-priority project on the first available day. If we do that, we will be productively managing our time to make good use of those valuable big blocks of time.

With the Children

Saturday hours are powerful because of all that we can accomplish during the day, but also because they allow us the opportunity to spend time with our children working and fellowshipping. I remember a basement remodel that I managed to complete over the course of numerous Saturdays. Two of my younger sons were about two and four when we started. We have some very precious photos of those little guys working furiously with their tool belts on and hammers in hand. They pounded untold numbers of nails into the footers of the walls of that basement. Of course, they weren't any real help at all, but did we ever enjoy working together. There were a few more interruptions than I would have had without their "help" because they would ask to hammer in a different place or if they could try something else. Anytime I had a project where I could, I would include not only my older sons, but also my younger ones as well.

In these recent years, I am experiencing the fruit of that investment. Together with my boys, we built first a shed, then a deck, and finally a whole house for our family. Right now we are in the midst of converting an old passenger bus into an RV on which our family can live when we are on the road speaking.

I have been at my computer writing this book while my fourteen-, eighteen-, and twenty-year-old sons are out working on the conversion. I am available to answer questions, oversee the work at regular intervals, and be a working companion on Saturdays. Because I have included them in the work I have done around the house through the years, they are capable of handling the big projects now that they are older. What is especially rewarding for me is they have certain skill sets where they can actually do better work than I can. What a blessing to see how my investment of time in their lives pays off.

> I have had a hard time in the past with home projects with the children because I am impatient. I felt like the work never got done, and they were slowing me down. I needed a change of heart on this. I have included my children on more projects lately, and it has been great.

Maybe you would tell me that you only have daughters. My girls supply the workers with drinks and snacks. They provide job-site cleanup, and they also work alongside of us. They pulled wire in the new house, cleaned grout, and helped with plumbing. Almost any task we undertook, they were helping us do it. As my girls work beside me and their brothers, they are learning to be a helpmeet in the future to a husband. They will have the attitudes and skills that should make them not only a physical help when a project comes along but also a blessing to their spouses.

We could have spent Saturdays hunting, fishing, watching ball games on TV, or playing computer games together. We would have been in physical proximity to each other. However, the skills my sons have gained by working with me, the appetites for wasting time that they have avoided, and our fellowship in the process are priceless to me. It has been worth every sacrifice I made for the outcome we have experienced. I want to encourage you in this path as well. You won't regret it, but will be blessed beyond measure by it.

Days Off Are Precious

The years pass quickly, and there are so few days off that we don't want to let them slip away. Whether Saturdays or holidays, these large blocks of time represent excellent opportunities to be with our families while accomplishing tasks that should be done. When we start the day prepared and with a plan in mind, we can be productive and efficient, making the most out of the hours we have at our disposal during these days. If we will get up early on Saturdays, we multiply the time we have available, and we will accomplish just that much more. Saturdays allow us to work with our children, teaching them lifelong, beneficial skills and character, while we disciple them and fellowship with them. May we be faithful stewards of the time God gives us by redeeming our time and learning to number our days.

Chapter 9

A Time for Worship and Rest

A discussion of time management for Christian men would not be complete without addressing Sundays. The utilization of these hours in our week is just as integral to our time management as are the normal work days. For most men, Sundays provide a second day away from the place of employment, and they will involve choices as to how that time will be spent. Once again we will either fritter Sunday's hours away, or we will seek the Lord Jesus for how He would have us to spend that time.

It would be good for me to make the point that this book is about time management, and it is not a doctrinal study on the Sabbath versus Sunday. I know respectable men of God have settled this issue different ways. Since a discussion on time management would have to touch on the subject of how Sundays are spent, I am going to share with you what our family has chosen, why, and how it affects what I do with my time on Sundays. You will base your decisions on what you see scripturally as your directives from the Lord Jesus for Sunday's time usage.

At First, Just Like Everyone Else

My upbringing was fairly traditional in that my family went to church off and on, and there was even a time when we attended pretty regularly. No one would have called us religious, though, because we knew how to keep religion in its proper place. To me, Sunday was not quite like all the other days, because there weren't any good shows on TV. Other than that, after church, it was all the same.

Teri and I were married in 1974. In 1975, I was saved and came into a real relationship with Jesus Christ. My heart was changed, and now I actually wanted to go to church and worship as opposed to being made to go like when I was a child. Meeting with brothers and sisters in Christ was totally different from the "religious duty" of just going to church. Sunday mornings and evenings we were at church, but Sunday afternoons were still much like Saturdays because I would have time to mow the lawn, take care of another project, or do something with the family.

We lived our life like that for over ten years following my salvation, and God gave us three children. He then introduced us to some biblical teaching that Sunday should be not only a day of worship but also a day of rest. Over time, as the Lord was working in our hearts and we were reading His Word daily, we felt that He was leading us to make Sunday different—more different than just going to church.

Isaiah 58:13-14, shown below, conveys the essence of what our family settled on as a blending of the Old Testament and the New Testament without the burden of going back under the law that Paul so clearly admonishes against in Galatians 3:2-3.

> "If thou turn away thy foot from the sabbath, *from* doing thy pleasure on my holy day; and call the sabbath a delight, the holy of the LORD, honourable; and shalt honour him, not doing thine own ways, nor finding thine own pleasure, nor speaking *thine own* words: Then shalt thou delight thyself in the LORD; and I will cause thee to ride upon the high places of the earth, and feed thee with the heritage of Jacob thy father: for the mouth of the LORD hath spoken *it*" (Isaiah 58:13-14).

We began to make Sunday our day of worship beyond simply attending church services. It was a special day for our family to honor our Lord throughout the whole day. We would choose not to follow our own preferences, but reverence the Lord with our time both in our hearts and actions. We have worship during our family Bible time every day, but Sunday is unique in that it is wholly dedicated to worship for the family without the normal distraction of work and daily activities. I base the decision for Sunday to be our day of worship on a number of Scriptures, such as the following that show that the first day of the week was the choice for the early church: Acts 20:7, 1 Corinthians 16:2, John 20:19.

> We studied this about 14 years ago and came to the same conclusion. It has been an incredible blessing. No one wants to go back to "just another day."

A Day of Worship

Most families will have a day when they attend church or have their home church. Traditionally, the New Testament church has its worship on Sundays. This means that Sundays produce their own schedules based on when we attend the worship service or services and how far away we live.

To arrive at church on time, you should have a Sunday morning time-management plan in place that has been developed by working with your wife. The younger your children are, the earlier you need to be up to be able to accomplish all that has to be done so that your family isn't late. Normally, on Sunday, I get up at the same time as I do the other days of the week. I have my time in the Word, and then we eat breakfast and go to church.

As the spiritual leader in your home, you can bless your wife by taking the lead on Sunday mornings, rising early enough to have time in the Word, and being a practical help with breakfast and getting the children ready for church. As you set the direction and lend a strong hand, the spirit of your family when you leave for church should be peaceful and happy rather than stressed and angry.

I have spoken with many families whose fellowship will meet from mid-morning until mid-afternoon. Each family will be unique in how much time is spent in corporate worship, so each family's schedule for the day will be different. The important thing is that the family worships. "Not forsaking the assembling of ourselves together, as the manner of some *is*; but exhorting *one another*: and so much the more, as ye see the day approaching" (Hebrews 10:25). May we have a joyous, edifying day worshipping the King of kings and Lord of lords each and every week.

Meetings with the Children

After we get home from church, I'm usually able to begin my meetings with each child around 11:30. That is an important and special time for the children and me because they afford the opportunity for one-on-one communication with an individual child. When lunch is ready, I take a break from the meetings. I will usually finish with the last child's meeting around 2:30 or 3:00.

Often a child will save up topics throughout the week that he wants to discuss with me, knowing he will have my undivided attention during our meeting. I want to maximize my time utilization even on Sundays. Since my Sunday focus is spiritual growth, the discipleship of my children fits well into my priorities and vision for my family. When something is important, it must be scheduled if it is going to happen consistently.

A Day of Rest

It is very clear the Lord's original plan was for man to work six days and rest on the seventh. "Six days may work be done;

I find it sad (and a little humorous) that God gives us a day of rest, but so few take it. When my employer gives me a day off, I take it. I am not going in to the office. Would people give up vacation days? Then why give up God's day of rest?

but in the seventh is the sabbath of rest, holy to the LORD. . ." (Exodus 31:15). As believers, we have chosen to follow the same reasoning and leading regarding working six days but then having a day of rest. The Hebrew word for Sabbath is *Shabbat*, and it means to rest. Therefore our family has chosen to make Sunday a day not only of worship but also of rest, even though the New Testament does not require it.

We plan our work projects for evenings and Saturdays, but we avoid them on Sundays. We prepare and clean up from meals, but we don't do any other household tasks on Sundays. We have seen how much easier it is to have a focus on the Lord Jesus with our Sundays when our minds aren't full of projects and plans, and we aren't hurrying to get to work on them. Sometimes busy dads are discouraged that they don't have more time to spend with the Lord and with their families. Sundays provide that time when we choose not to do work projects.

Sundays, as days of rest, also allow us the opportunity for some extra sleep in the afternoon. Following my meetings with the children, we all take naps. The length of time each sleeps varies and is based on how much sleep they have found they need. Teri and I will sleep a maximum of two hours because we have discovered that rest to be helpful for us, preparing us to begin the new week refreshed. I also believe my two-hour Sunday nap allows me to get by with a little less sleep each night during the week.

A Day of Study

Sundays provide me with time for in-depth Bible study. During the week, I have personal and family time in the Word every day. However, I also desire to be able to get out the concordance, expository dictionary, and a commentary or two to dig into the Word. This is for my personal growth and edification, but it also is imparting to me biblical knowledge that I can pass on to my family.

I think that if you will work your time-management plan to allow you a weekly Bible-study time, you will find yourself excited by what you learn in the Word. "All scripture *is* given by inspiration of God, and *is* profitable for doctrine, for reproof, for correction, for instruction in righteousness: That the man of God may be perfect, throughly furnished unto all good works" (2 Timothy 3:16-17). You will be able to teach your children more easily. "But grow in grace, and *in* the knowledge of our Lord and Saviour Jesus Christ. . ." (2 Peter 3:18). As your knowledge of the Lord Jesus grows through your study of Scripture, you are becoming furnished for all good works, including how to redeem the time and number your days.

Not Our Own Pleasure

Our family has also set a high priority of not "doing thy pleasure" on our day of worship and rest, as found in Isaiah 58:13: "If thou turn away thy foot from the sabbath, *from* doing thy pleasure on my holy day; and call the sabbath a delight, the holy of the LORD, honourable; and shalt honour him, not doing thine own ways, nor finding thine own pleasure, nor speaking *thine own* words." The Hebrew for "pleasure" is *hepes* and according to *Strong's Talking Greek and Hebrew Dictionary* it means "acceptable, delight, desire, pleasant." We are to delight in doing the things in which the Lord delights and not those in which our flesh may take pleasure. For our family, we have chosen on Sundays not to do the following: go out to eat, go shopping, pursue recreational activities, be entertained, work around the house, or conduct any business. There are only a few exceptions to this for us. An example would be when we are on a conference-speaking trip and eat out on a Sunday.

What we do is worship the Lord, assemble with believers, rest, read and study His Word, fellowship together as a family around His Word, take walks, and talk on the deck or in the living room. We love our Sundays together as family time centered on the Lord Jesus.

The Battle Rages

The flesh will fight furiously against the Spirit over how Sunday is spent. There will be pressure from well-meaning friends and extended family for us to participate in a myriad of non-edifying activities. Certainly, the world would embrace the idea of spending Sunday in front of the TV.

For several years after becoming a Christian, I didn't have my quiet time on Sunday morning with the justification that I would be in the Word at church. After repenting of that poor choice, I now see how important being in the Word on Sunday morning is for preparing my heart to worship the Lord. I'm not saying a person can't worship on Sunday if he hasn't had his quiet time, but I am confident being in the Lord's presence first will greatly enhance one's corporate worship.

Be advised and expect the flesh to seek his own way, but be determined to make choices surrendered to the leadership of the Lord. I believe that giving the Lord Jesus Christ first priority in my time has been the key to having peace and victory over struggles with time. "But seek ye first the kingdom of God, and his righteousness; and all these things shall be added unto you" (Matthew 6:33).

However, I believe the opposite to be true as well. If we as children of the Lord give our time to "another," we can expect difficulties and even consequences for it. As you read Scripture, watch how the Lord allows chastening similar to the offense. In this case, the analogy would mean that if we take time the Lord has directed to be used in one area and give it to "the flesh," we can expect time consequences.

When Israel strayed from the Lord, giving their time and attention to other gods, the Lord sent in the nations who worshipped those gods to rule over them. "And they forsook the LORD, and served Baal and Ashtaroth. And the anger of the LORD was hot against Israel, and he delivered them into the hands of spoilers that spoiled them, and he sold them into the hands of their enemies round about, so that they could not any longer stand before their enemies" (Judges 2:13-14). God was saying that if they wouldn't serve Him, they would serve others.

Sunday's Choices

Sundays afford us time for corporate worship plus physical and spiritual rest. When we set a day aside each week and let go of our normal activities, our minds and bodies can regroup in preparation for the upcoming week. Without the distractions of our usual vocational work and home tasks, we have the freedom to focus our hearts more fully on the Lord Jesus Christ. Sundays are a precious time for both spiritual and physical refreshing. May we serve the Lord Jesus as He directs and receive the accompanying rest He gives. "Come unto me, all *ye* that labour and are heavy laden, and I will give you rest. Take my yoke upon you, and learn of me; for I am meek and lowly in heart: and ye shall find rest unto your souls. For my yoke *is* easy, and my burden is light" (Matthew 11:28-30). Each of us has a decision to make. How will we spend our time—as the Lord directs or after the dictates of the flesh?

His Time Is Her Time

A key aspect of time management for a married man will be the time investment he makes in his relationship with his wife and in helping her when particular needs arise that are beyond her scope to solve. If one wants to build that relationship, it will take time. If one wants to meet those needs, it will take time. Managing our time will allow for this important area of our lives. It is simply another part of redeeming the time and learning to number our days.

Flat Tire

There is a section of I-64 between Richmond and Virginia Beach, Virginia, where the pavement has many small, long grooves. The children had been noticing them as we drove along and asked me about them. I explained that those grooves were likely from boat trailers that had a flat tire, and the wheel would have worn through the tire until the rim was dragging along the payment. The RV pulling it would have been unaware of the problem; therefore, the driver would have just kept heading for the destination, not realizing that his trailer had a serious problem. We've seen this happen with eighteen-wheelers, when the driver didn't know that a trailer tire was flat. If undetected, the tire can catch fire. We flagged down a truck driver near Huntsville one night because he was unaware of what was happening. His tire was smoking very badly due to the friction.

A similar situation occurs in homes when the dad is so focused on what he wants to be doing that he fails to notice that the one "hitched" to him is struggling and in serious trouble. Mom may have a "flat tire," needing some attention and help, but Dad is determined to get where he wants to go, not wanting to take time to stop. Dad just continues on, and poor Mom is being "dragged down the road behind him," sometimes smoking due to the friction. Others near the couple may be aware of the problem and try to flag Dad down to help him understand, but he keeps right on going.

An example of this concerning my wife occurred when we had several little children, were homeschooling, and Teri was struggling with depression. At that time I was asked to be the president of the Kansas state homeschool association and the chairman of the local branch of an international ministry. I agreed to take both positions. While Teri sat home with most of the children and cried, I was busy serving the Lord. Teri was about as flat as she could get. The Lord used experiences like this and His Word to begin to open my eyes to the importance of being heedful of the needs of my wife. "Husbands, love your wives, even as Christ also loved the church, and gave himself for it" (Ephesians 5:25).

A Team

Dad is not to be a "Lone Ranger" once he takes a bride. "For this cause shall a man leave his father and mother, and shall be joined unto his wife, and they two shall be one flesh" (Ephesians 5:31). Some might ask what that has to do with a time management book for men. For the Christian man, the answer is: everything. Once a man has a wife, God's plan is that they become one in body, soul, and spirit. A husband's life is no

> There are times when a lot of time and energy is needed to care for a wife. That should be expected and honored. A wife is a big responsibility and also a great blessing. "In sickness and health?" Both? Yes!

longer his only, but it is totally joined with his wife's. One aspect of this relationship is that a Christian husband's time is not his own but is shared with his wife, and directed by the Lord Jesus.

"I am not sure about how to answer a couple of the questions because my husband doesn't tell me things and ministers in his own way without me knowing or agreeing at times. I wish he would share why he does what he does and not get offended by my questions."

How sad to be in a relationship that the Lord has designed to be a team, and have one who isn't communicating and becoming offended if there are questions.

Peter made it very clear how the husband must have a constant ear to his wife. "Likewise, ye husbands, dwell with *them* according to knowledge, giving honour unto the wife, as unto the weaker vessel, and as being heirs together of the grace of life; that your prayers be not hindered" (1 Peter 3:7). We are to live with a wife according to knowledge. It is to be a rational, thought-out life. We are to understand her needs as the weaker vessel

> I set aside time on Sunday to review the week with my wife —listen to her plans, goals, desires, concerns, and frustrations. It's a valuable time for me to see where she needs my help and lets her know I'm here for her.

and to meet those needs. That will have to be accounted for in our time management.

Our wives' interest in our time is further supported in the following two verses. "Let the husband render unto the wife due benevolence: and likewise also the wife unto the husband.

The wife hath not power of her own body, but the husband: and likewise also the husband hath not power of his own body, but the wife" (1 Corinthians 7:3-4). Clearly these verses refer to the physical relationship as a primary application, but it has secondary application on the subject of a husband's time. The husband and wife each have a voice in the life of the other as to how that life is lived out. Yes, the husband is the head, but there is a mutual submission consistent with Ephesians 5:21: "Submitting yourselves one to another in the fear of God."

The husband's time and the wife's time are possessed by each other, totally intertwined with each other. They are yoked together. "Be ye not unequally yoked together with unbelievers: for what fellowship hath righteousness with unrighteousness? and what communion hath light with darkness?" (2 Corinthians 6:14). Our time, which is the most precious aspect of our life, is jointly shared in ownership with our wives.

A husband and wife are a team under the leadership of the Lord to do as the Lord directs, and that is where so many dads get into trouble. They have listened to the dictates of the "urgent," left the Lord's direction, and forgotten about the needs of the one with whom they are yoked. It will take good communication with a wife, prayer, and a time investment to prevent her from feeling like that flat tire being dragged down life's highway behind her husband.

Sensitive to Her Needs

There have been times when I looked at Teri's needs as a hindrance to my getting things done. If I was spending time on her concerns or projects, I couldn't take care of mine. I have to admit that I considered her needs less important and an unnecessary weight that became a source of frustration and pressure. Proof of such an attitude is whose needs get top priority. That attitude is not consistent with 1 Peter 3:7. She is the weaker vessel, and I am called to understand her needs, bearing them even to the point of the cross. "Husbands, love your wives, even as Christ also loved the church, and gave himself for it" (Ephesians 5:25). Christ not only gave His life for His bride, the church, but He also lived His life self-sacrificially for her while He was alive. This is our calling as well.

One example from my life where God called me to sacrificially serve Teri and the family beyond what is normally needed was just after we had a baby. Our midwife suggested that Teri stay in bed for a week after each delivery for rest and bonding with the baby. I put my agenda aside, took a week of vacation, and cared for the family for the week. Those weeks were so good for enhancing my appreciation for all Teri does. As we surrender our lives and time to the Lord, He will build our families up and glorify Himself. I wouldn't trade those times for anything.

> *"My husband is self-employed. Work has always been a priority for him. I will say that I have learned about work ethic from him, but I do have to work on my patience as far as him having time with his family (or lack of it) goes. He and I have made life changes in order to make it possible for me to remain home with the children, but I fear that all too often I end up taking on more than what might be healthy for a homeschooling mom (expecting number six)."*

We must be cautious if we are asking our wives for help with a home business, ministry, or areas of our home responsibility. A mom has a great amount of work to do in caring for a husband, children, and home, and even more if she is homeschooling. Far better that we were relieving her of her load than adding to it. In order to do this, we have to learn to manage our own time rather than handing off responsibilities to our wives.

As husband and wife, we are to face each day as a team, with the Lord as our teamster, and be committed to obeying His direction. If we do, we can expect how we manage our time to include many of our wives' needs, and there will be great blessings in the process.

An Eye on the Future

When Teri brings me a problem, it will have an impact on my time. I can choose to ignore it, put it off, or make it a priority. I have learned from experience that there is great blessing to Teri, my family, and to myself when I take her needs seriously and budget time for them.

I remember a year when Teri was struggling with laying out a new schedule. We had eight children, six of whom she was homeschooling (the other two were too young). She had them on a schedule each year, but there were a number of reasons why that particular year was very difficult for her to figure out the schedule. One of the reasons for her scheduling struggles was that we only had one mama, one computer, and one piano. There were a number of children who needed to use those resources at nonconflicting times. Teri was frustrated and asked for help.

I sat down with her and tried to work through some of the options. I soon understood the problem she was having and had a suggestion. I proposed she put the tasks on little pieces of paper that she could move around like puzzle pieces until it worked out. Amazingly, those thirty minutes I invested with her have blessed her every year since then as she puts together her schedule. Not only that, but God then used that scheduling idea He gave us as a portion of the *Managers of Their Homes* resource, which has helped tens of thousands of moms.

I believe God will multiply our investment of time when we yield it to Him. Helping relieve our wives of problems will cost us some time right away, but it will save a great deal of time in the long run. In addition, there are innumerable benefits in a husband-and-wife relationship when a husband takes a problem that his wife brings to him seriously and helps her solve it. I think each time I do this, Teri not only thanks me but also tells me how much she loves me. Remember those value bucks? When I invest my time toward relieving Teri's need and build our relationship in the process, I feel like I do when I spend those value bucks!

Helping Her Be Successful

When things are not going well in the home, there will be a great amount of "damage control" needed on our part. If we have not shouldered our responsibilities and invested the necessary time to raise the children in the nurture and admonition of the Lord, they will be undisciplined and difficult to manage, requiring much extra time and energy. We must own the fact that we are the ones God is holding accountable; therefore, we must invest the time required.

> During the first years of homeschooling, I refused to help my wife plan the school year, schedule, or curriculum. I would say it was her job, because I was unwilling to work with her. Our homeschooling jumped from one curriculum to another almost every year. I was not confident that the children were getting the most out of their education. It has been a lot better once I took the time to plan and help her with homeschool decisions.

Occasionally we hear from a mom who had been crying out to her husband that there are problems, and he has told her he was just too busy to help. Other moms share that when the dad does try to help, he only gives a little bit of time instead of dealing with the root issues.

In Kansas we have these pretty, yellow flowers that come up in lawns every spring—dandelions. I've seen them quickly take over a lawn. One possible solution is to pick the flowers off so they can't go to seed, preventing further spreading. However, dandelions are so prolific, they keep putting out new flowers at a rapid-fire pace. One would have to keep running around the yard every day picking off the flowers to prevent it from getting worse. Instead of picking flowers, now consider if Dad would spend extra time using a special tool digging out the whole weed and most of the root. Even better is to take a little more time to squirt weed killer into the hole from which the weed was removed. The crux of the problem is how to convince dads to stop running around frantically pulling off the tops of dandelions and put their time and effort into what is really needed. Do you get the picture? The root problem lies below the surface, and that is where the real time and attention must be focused.

Eli did not take the time necessary to train up his sons in the way they should go. He might have reasoned that he was too busy serving the Lord. Who could have a better use of time? Right? Or so one thinks. We see clearly the Lord did not agree. "For I have told him that I will judge his house for ever for the iniquity which he knoweth; because his sons made themselves vile, and he restrained them not" (1 Samuel 3:13). I have spoken with many dads consumed with "ministry" while the greatest ministry God has called them to is a lower priority and doesn't receive Dad's time. "If any be blameless, the husband of one wife, having faithful children not accused of riot or unruly" (Titus 1:6). The Lord holds us accountable for our wives and children. We are the spiritual heads of our homes. Our wives know the needs of the family, but often Dad doesn't listen to the cries for help—he's too busy.

When the children are undisciplined, everything Mom tries to do with them will take longer. The children will be slow about finishing their chores, and what they do will be done poorly. Some moms find it easier to do all the housework themselves than to battle the children to get them to help. Schoolwork becomes so difficult that untold numbers of moms finally cave in and plead with Dad to send the children to school. These unnecessary problems that Mom faces will be shared with Dad, who will search for solutions on a per-instance basis. This will take a great deal more of Dad's time than if the problems had been prevented in the first place. How much better it is to invest the time to disciple the children and have home life be a blessing for all concerned! The end result is that it will take far less of Dad's time once he begins investing in discipling and training the children. Two resources that may be helpful to your family in this area are *Managers of Their Chores* and *Managers of Their Schools*. Included in each book is a chapter I wrote for dads. We continue to hear many testimonies from moms whose families have been blessed by both books.

There could be many areas where a mom needs Dad's help, such as the following: grading schoolwork, teaching a subject, helping organize, making curriculum decisions, washing dishes, or putting the children to bed. Whatever the need is, are we willing to step in? Anything our wives do is one less thing we need to do. Dad may think he doesn't have time to help his wife, but it is our reasonable service to enable her to be successful.

"I am blessed with a wonderful husband. He works out of our home and has to travel 10-15 nights a year. He manages most of our homeschooling. I just have the younger ones until they can read and write well. He assigns, corrects, and I just have to make sure it gets done throughout the day. He does a Bible study and Scripture memory with all the children and also reads a chapter book at night. He is very active with our chil-

dren, playing with them, doing yard work, and ministering.
I feel extremely blessed to be married to him."

Here is a dad who is a joy to his wife and his children. He has learned to number his days, redeem the time, and he is investing that time as the Lord Jesus would have him to. He is making his wife successful.

How's the Flow?

I mentioned earlier about the problem that RVs have when they have a "toad." That is a term used to refer to a towed vehicle. It is a real and challenging problem for which to find a solution. The large, ninety-six-inch-wide motor homes have no way to observe a flat tire on the narrower toad because they usually can't see what they are towing via their rearview mirrors. Even if they have a backup camera, the camera won't show them the status of the tires. A tire can go flat, and from the camera's angle above, it looks fine. Only once the smoke starts to rise from a disintegrated tire and hot rim being dragged along pavement would they see it. The best solution for this problem is installing a tire-monitoring system that is available for the toad's tires. It feeds information to the RV driver concerning the condition of the tires.

Dad needs a similar monitoring system. It is necessary for Dad to receive a constant, accurate status from Mom and the children. What is she seeing in the lives of the children that needs to be addressed? What influences are causing Mom concern? What are the attitudes and behaviors of the children? Is the family on course with the vision God has given for them? If not, what sort of corrections should be made to get back on course? Does Dad want to know, and does he desire to address these real issues?

Building relationships and communication takes time. For years Teri and I had a weekly date night. Before our oldest child was old enough to babysit, we hired a babysitter while we went out to eat. We were able to discuss whatever was on Teri's heart. She usually had a list of things so she wouldn't forget them. One by one, we would step through her list, and she would write down the answers.

For the past several years, Teri and I have walked together early in the mornings after our personal time in the Word before I start work. This is part of my time-management plan. The walking doubles for exercise and communication. During our walks, Teri and I have time to talk about the many needs and aspects of our lives. While we greatly enjoyed our weekly dates, daily walks are much better suited for keeping up with the communication that facilitates a closer relationship.

A husband and wife going away for a night or two is excellent for relationship building, including discussion time without distractions. I have made this a priority in my time management and financial planning since the beginning of our marriage. When the children were little, it cost me time to find reliable care for them while we were away in addition to the actual time we were gone. As I would watch Teri's face and heart when we had those snippets of time away from her normal, daily responsibilities, it made it worth every hour and dollar I spent.

Just like a system to monitor tires on a toad, good communication will cost something. We must allow time to ensure that the lines of communication are wide open and that we are resolving the issues that surface.

It's a War—Not with Mom, But with the Flesh

We must be on guard for the flesh warring against us to keep us from doing the right thing. "For if ye live after the flesh, ye shall die: but if ye through the Spirit do mortify the deeds of the body, ye shall live" (Romans 8:13). Instead of guarding our wife's time or spending time helping her, our flesh will selfishly pile more work onto her already-heavy load. Instead of spending time discipling our children as our wives' hearts cry out for, we will take some time merely to correct a child before rushing off to tackle the next "fire."

We need to spend time listening carefully to our wives. We must take what they say before the Lord, and then use the time necessary to deal with the root problems. Our time is her time, and we must follow the Lord's direction.

CHAPTER

11

Time for Ministry

A book for Christian men on time management would be remiss if it didn't include a chapter about managing ministry time. Considering how precious time is, this should be discussed. Twenty-seven percent of the families who responded to our survey reported that the dad ministered outside the home somewhere each week. It is possible some may not be ministering when the Lord would have them to, and others might be doing this when they should be home with their families. Either one is just as counterproductive with its negative impact on the family.

Ministry Defined

I have heard the word "ministry" used in many ways so for the sake of clarity, let's define it. The Greek word *diakonia*, translated as "ministry, ministration, ministering, serving, relief, office, and administrations," is used thirty-two times in the New Testament. A beginning definition could simply be "some form of Christian service." The problem with that definition would lie in the word "Christian," which is not a good adjective since Christian can

> I used to play in the worship team on Sunday. That required a 3-hour Monday night practice and getting to church on Sunday before my family. This was too costly for me.

mean different things to different people. Let's then refine the definition a step further, as follows: "service done in the name and at the direction of the Lord Jesus to sustain and build up others physically or spiritually." That could encompass everything from helping a widow by raking her leaves to serving at church, as long as it was directed by the Lord Jesus.

We are called to service, and Jesus set the example in giving His life for others. "Then said Jesus unto his disciples, If any *man* will come after me, let him deny himself, and take up his cross, and follow me" (Matthew 16:24). Our time is so precious. It is critical that we are serving when and where Jesus directs us to serve.

First Ministry Priority

Do you remember what God told Samuel about Eli in 1 Samuel 3:13? "For I have told him that I will judge his house for ever for the iniquity which he knoweth; because his sons made themselves vile, and he restrained them not." Eli was a priest and judged Israel. He had a very important position. He was chosen of God for that ministry. Did God forget that He had chosen Eli for that position? Wasn't that ministry more important than raising children in the nurture and admonition of the Lord? NO! No to both questions. Once God gives us children, they become our first ministry, our vital priority in life. They are more important than our careers and our other ministries. Eli's family would be judged FOREVER because of Eli's unfaithfulness to his family.

If time preference is given to "ministry" outside the home over family, a dad teaches his children to ignore their future families. This also often leads to rebellion in children—they feel Dad doesn't love them.

I believe Eli's example is critical to understanding that our first ministry priority is raising our children in the nurture and admonition of the Lord. Then in time, as we prove ourselves faithful in that task, the Lord will add other opportunities to serve that will build up and strengthen the family in the process.

Some might argue that ministering is more important than raising a family. They might even claim children are a hindrance to serving and quote Jesus' words about what is more important: "If any *man* come to me, and hate not his father, and mother, and wife, and children, and brethren, and sisters, yea, and his own life also, he cannot be my disciple" (Luke 14:26). Now compare that to what Jesus said to the rich young ruler: "Honour thy father and *thy* mother: and, Thou shalt love thy neighbour as thyself" (Matthew 19:19). How can we hate our father and mother and yet honor them? Luke 14:26 is one of those times when Jesus was giving an exaggerated comparison. Jesus is saying our love for Him is to be so great, it would be as if we hated our parents. We are not to hate our parents or our children, but rather we are to love the Lord Jesus more than we love them.

While Jesus was on the cross, at the time when the real work of the ministry of the apostles was just about to begin, He did something quite strange. "When Jesus therefore saw his mother, and the disciple standing by, whom he loved, he saith unto his mother, Woman, behold thy son! Then saith he to the disciple, Behold thy mother! And from that hour that disciple took her unto his own *home*" (John 19:26-27). Why would Jesus do that when His mother had other children who could have seen to her needs? Why would Jesus burden John with the care of Jesus' mother, when John needed to be busy with the work of an apostle? We can't know Jesus' motives, but we can see that a portion of John's ministry would involve caring for

Jesus' mother. When Jesus directs us to serve in various ways, it will not be to the detriment of our family.

Does It Build Up Your Family?

Building up the family is a key point to consider when evaluating whether a "ministry opportunity" is truly heaven sent or of earthly origin. In fact, I believe any ministry sent from the Lord will enable us to build up the family, sharpening and equipping them to serve. As dads we need to understand that our credentials for service are stated in 1 Timothy 3:4: "One that ruleth well his own house, having his children in subjection with all gravity." If we aren't raising our children in the nurture and admonition of the Lord, we shouldn't consider any other ministry outside the home, no matter how passionate the plea is for help. How well we raise our children in the Lord is an important qualification for additional serving.

> I always felt like my wife was not understanding the importance of my church ministry, but the reality is I was not understanding the vital importance of first ministering to my family. I have repented and asked my wife to forgive me for the years I put them second or third.

A young, discouraged pastor shared with me that he was told by a denomination that after completing seminary he would be expected to work fifty to sixty hours a week and at times more than that. His young family would have to be second to the needs of the church. Is it any wonder that so many pastors lose their children? I remember a pastor coming up to me after a conference. His part of the conversation went like this: "Preach it, brother. I lost my daughter to the world because of my church. I spent too much time involved in church responsibilities and not enough with my family."

Since one of the qualifications for leadership is having faithful children, God would not call a man to a ministry that would result in him losing his children. "If any be blameless, the husband of one wife, having faithful children not accused of riot or unruly" (Titus 1:6). We can expect, though, to be called to a ministry where our family will be built up and used. "As arrows *are* in the hand of a mighty man; so *are* children of the youth" (Psalms 127:4). If God gives us children, He intends to use them as arrows in the father's bow.

Bringing our children up in the nurture and admonition of the Lord is our foremost goal. That will take our time, and while we are discipling our children, we can't be doing other things by ourselves. However, I discovered that there were many ministry opportunities that I could do with our children. This allowed me to serve while discipling our children and giving them a hunger for serving. Teri and I led our local home-school support group for ten years. Our children worked right alongside us. As I mentioned previously, we have ministered at a local nursing home and at a homeless mission. We use hospitality for family ministry as well.

I wonder if my heart to obey the Lord by desiring to put my family as my first priority for ministry and then seeking ways to serve with them is what the Lord has used to allow me the ministry opportunities I now have. If a dad will invest the gifts and talents the Lord has given him into his family and find ministries he can do with them, there will be a time when his children are "sharp and straight" and ready to be used by the Lord. Then the dad's ministry capabilities will far surpass anything he could have done on his own.

Positive and Negative Examples

Since it is vitally important that fathers come to view their families as their most important ministry rather than separating family from ministry, I want to share with you some real-life stories. Here are two examples of dads who have learned this truth and are applying it in their lives.

"My husband doesn't minister outside the home because his time is so precious with his family."

"The Lord has graciously brought my husband to a place in his life where he understands that the relationship he has with the Lord is the KEY! We have been blessed with eleven children, and my husband views them as a huge ministry opportunity. He pours intentional time and energy into them daily. It is truly a blessing to have a husband that loves the Lord, obeys His Word, and leads our family accordingly."

Now evaluate with me two fathers who are pursuing non-family ministries, and consider the outcomes these families may experience.

"He keeps up with everything, but has trouble spending enough time with our eight children most weeks. He wants to be involved with homeschooling, but generally isn't, other than 'Bible time' with the family which is sporadic, as well as family meals. He teaches a large adult Sunday School class and struggles to find time to prepare for teaching as well as minister to the needs of the families in the class. It is much like a small church within the church. He also teaches a small Bible study at work during lunch once a week."

"My husband is not only a deacon in our church, but also he is a Sunday School teacher and the chairman of the finance committee. This can take up to nine hours of his time on Sundays at least twice a month."

What do you think will be the spiritual outcome in the lives of the children in these four families? I am convinced that the fathers who view their children as a ministry will have children who excitedly choose to follow the Lord Jesus wholeheartedly, just as they see their father doing. However, the fathers who are not ministering to their families as they should are likely to experience the heartbreak of children who have little or no desire to serve the Lord. The lack of spiritual teaching and leadership they will experience, coupled with the bitterness over not having a father involved in their lives, has great potential to turn their hearts away from both the family and Jesus Christ.

Is It God's Will?

I'm sure there are whole books written on finding and obeying God's will. A lengthy discussion of that would be far beyond the scope of a book on time management, but some mention seems critical to helping readers understand God's will for their time. Therefore it will suffice to briefly share several key points I have come to rely on when trying to discern God's will. I have found that a number of "witnesses" are reliable in helping me to avoid some of the mistakes I've made previously in missing God's will. I will briefly expand on each item.

Consistent with His Word—Since Jesus is the Living Word, what He directs us to do will be consistent with Scripture. The only way we will know that is by being in the Word every day with a heart to know and apply it to our lives. "Thy word *is* a lamp unto my feet, and a light unto my path" (Psalms 119:105).

Obedience—This is critical to knowing God's will. Have we responded obediently to His will previously? Have we proven ourselves faithful in little? God uses our obedience to develop an understanding of whether something is from the Lord. "If any man will do his will, he shall know of the doctrine, whether it be of God, or *whether* I speak of myself" (John 7:17).

Fruit—This is a powerful way to know whether something is of God. What fruit in general and in the family will result from this decision? "For every tree is known by his own fruit.

For of thorns men do not gather figs, nor of a bramble bush gather they grapes" (Luke 6:44).

Wife's Counsel—This is very important to have heard and then brought before the Lord. From my experience, sometimes it is good, and other times it is inconsistent with God's will. However, it has always been beneficial to have heard my wife's heart. Adam got into trouble because he obeyed Eve. He should have listened carefully to her and then taken everything to the Lord for direction. Often our wives will see things we miss and need to hear. "Submitting yourselves one to another in the fear of God" (Ephesians 5:21).

Consistent with Our Vision—This is a test of whether God is leading. Is the direction down the same path as the vision God has previously given? "A double minded man *is* unstable in all his ways" (James 1:8).

Current Performance—This is a good indication of whether it is the Lord bringing more for us to do. If we aren't wise stewards currently of the time He gives us, we shouldn't expect the Lord to add to our responsibilities. "Moreover it is required in stewards, that a man be found faithful" (1 Corinthians 4:2).

Prayer—This is that critical link to the Father where we share our hearts and hear His. It isn't enough that we send up an occasional flare prayer; we must be having a daily time of communication with the Father. Then when challenging issues come up, we have experience in hearing and knowing the voice of our Lord. "My sheep hear my voice, and I know them, and they follow me" (John 10:27).

Not God's Will

Over twenty years ago, the head of a large, para-church organization told me on the phone late one night, "I believe it

This has caused me trouble before too. We need to always seek God's will for ourselves.

is God's will that you take this position I am offering to you." Wow, what an honor, and who could possibly refuse? Here was someone older, wiser, and more mature in the Lord telling me what God's will was for my life.

After hastily praying about it, I agreed that it was God's will, and so I accepted this important volunteer position with great anticipation. I began to pour my heart and life into my new responsibilities. Then to my shock, in less than a month, this man's assistant was calling me and asking me to resign. I was devastated and brokenhearted. Looking back, it is clear it wasn't God's will that I take that position in the first place. There was a need, and I was asked to fill it, but I was the wrong person.

Had I known then the criteria the Lord has since shown me about discerning His will, perhaps I wouldn't have made the wrong decision. If I had understood the importance of my family being my number-one ministry, maybe I wouldn't have been convinced to take a wrong turn. I know that my years of spiritual growth have made a difference in my ability to discern God's leading in my life. These witnesses for finding God's will have been taught to me by the Lord Jesus through His Word and a desire to obediently follow it. I believe the same can be true for any father who will make those same choices.

Be wary when a ministry opportunity comes along. So often this is what happens with a dad. He loves the Lord Jesus and wants to serve Him in whatever way He calls, and then along comes someone in a church or ministry who needs help. This poor dad is already "maxed out" with every available minute, and now there is the plea for his help. He assumes it is the Lord asking him to do it. Who can refuse the Lord's calling? However, it might not be the Lord's calling, but rather someone who needs a body to fill a position. Be faithful in your vital priority of discipling your children. Evaluate ministry opportunities based on whether you can involve your children and how it will impact your time with them. Look for those types of ministries in which you could serve with them. Be willing to say "no," for a season, to those ministries that will pull you away from your family.

How to Implement

Once we have peace that something is God's will, the next step is integrating it into our daily life. Because time is so precious and there are a host of other responsibilities to be kept up, finding the appropriate time in the schedule is important.

For around ten years, our family held a bimonthly nursing home service on Saturday afternoons. Also for ten years the Maxwell men went to a homeless shelter and had a service the second Saturday of each month. As I look back, I'm amazed at all the Lord allowed our family to accomplish on Saturdays in addition to the ministry commitments. Those ministries were good for the growth of the family, and the Lord has used that in equipping us to serve today.

We need to carefully evaluate the time we have available. It may be that a ministry opportunity can fit into a weekday evening or once a month. For the last year we were in Seattle, we ministered to a widow every Wednesday night instead of sending the children to the church's children's program that involved Scripture memory and lots of wild games. We loved our widow ministry. We had the blessing of ministering to the widow in exchange for the children not developing an appetite for the games. If ministry impacts family Bible time, then for that one day, Bible time could be held in the morning before work. May each of us be determined in our resolution not to let other things preclude our family Bible time. If it does, one would question whether the ministry opportunity is the Lord's will.

If it must be done on a Saturday, then the beginning or end of the day is best because it still leaves a big slice of time available for other endeavors. For our family, both the nursing home and mission ministries occurred right around lunchtime. That really impacted productivity for the rest of the day. Looking back, I have no regrets, but only gratefulness for how the Lord used and blessed us during those years. I do know that if I could do it over again, I would prefer to have scheduled the nursing home service earlier in the day. The homeless shelter service was for their noontime meal, and that could not have been moved.

Not If But When

When the Lord calls a family to minister to others, there will be time in the schedule to do it. The difficulty is first determining that the Lord is the One sending the opportunity to serve. Once you are sure it is the Lord's will, then it is simply a matter of fitting it into the schedule. The Lord Jesus requires fruit of all His children. "Ye have not chosen me, but I have chosen you, and ordained you, that ye should go and bring forth fruit, and *that* your fruit should remain: that whatsoever ye shall ask of the Father in my name, he may give it you" (John 15:16). He set the example, and if we are following Him, He will lead us to deny ourselves and minister to others. "Then said Jesus unto his disciples, If any *man* will come after me, let him deny himself, and take up his cross, and follow me" (Matthew 16:24). Jesus gave the ultimate in service for others on the cross in denying Himself. He has asked us to follow Him. Let's make the most of every ministry minute by serving others as a family.

Prune Out the Time Robbers

As we continue to delve into time management for busy Christian men, we want to address the critical area of time robbers. This chapter may present the most difficult information, but it also has the potential of being the most beneficial concerning time management. It is possible that many will discover things they cherish are nothing more than time robbers. Activities that have been embraced could be deceitfully stealing your most precious possession—your time. Now you will have the opportunity to begin acquiring it back.

Since our church is in a nursing home, we see many people who are right on the edge of eternity. At that point, there is nothing that can be done to redeem lost time. The thing that becomes most important during the later years of life are family relationships. Often we see beautiful families where the elderly parent is obviously loved. Other times, it is a heartbreak when the "child" lives in the area but doesn't care enough to pay even a token visit to see Dad or Mom in the nursing home. Could it be that if Dad had learned to number his days, there would have been the time to invest in that child, and the relationship could have been vastly different? This chapter is key to evaluating time robbers and banishing them from our lives. May each take a deep breath and be willing to be vulnerable as we expose time robbers.

Who Recognizes a Time Robber?

What most dads don't realize is that their wives and sometimes their children are aware that Dad is making poor decisions and squandering his time. Dad loses respect in their eyes, and it becomes difficult for his family to follow him. However, if Dad will prune out the time robbers by making wise decisions, I believe he will win the hearts of his family, and they will follow him as Israel followed David. "And David behaved himself wisely in all his ways; and the LORD *was* with him. Wherefore when Saul saw that he behaved himself very wisely, he was afraid of him. But all Israel and Judah loved David, because he went out and came in before them" (1 Samuel 18:14-16). It is easier for a family to love and follow a dad who is committed to following the Lord and not making selfish choices for how he will use his time.

However, be forewarned, when you finally recognize your time robbers and try to remove them from your life, they will turn on you and grab you by the throat. As hard as you try, you will have trouble shaking "them" loose. "Love not the world, neither the things *that are* in the world. If any man love the world, the love of the Father is not in him. For all that *is* in the world, the lust of the flesh, and the lust of the eyes, and the pride of life, is not of the Father, but is of the world" (1 John 2:15-16). Leaving the world is never easy because of the hold it has on our flesh.

The extreme examples of breaking free of drugs, alcohol, and tobacco everyone understands to be difficult. But let me tell you, these time robbers will give even "tough" guys the shakes. I've seen it in conferences where a dad will come up and agree something should go out of his life. He will stammer and struggle, trying to say he will get rid of it. You would think he was committing to cutting off an arm or something worse. I plead with you to have an open mind as you read this chapter. It will cost you nothing, and you can gain time, respect from your family, and peace from time pressure.

The Christian Norm

There is a popular mindset that while we Christians are on earth we are to serve the Lord, and we can choose to enjoy our time by pursuing non-sinful activities. The thought is that as long as the Lord hasn't told us "no" regarding something, then it is okay to do it because we are free in Christ.

I wonder how many Christian parents would exercise that same concept of "all is acceptable unless I have told you no" in their child rearing. Of course they wouldn't, because that would mean everything is permissible for their children unless Dad and Mom have explicitly commanded the child not to do it. "Don't play in the middle of any street in our town, our state, or our country. Don't play with our kitchen knives. Don't drink gasoline, kerosene, or diesel fuel. Oh, I forgot aviation fuel, don't drink that either. Don't drink furniture polish, paint thinner, lye . . ." The list would have to go on forever. It is absurd, and even if you thought to warn them of every danger, they would never remember such a long list. If we don't raise our children that way with our earthly wisdom, how could we ever think the Lord would choose that for us in His heavenly wisdom?

With the mindset that we can do whatever we please as long as it isn't sinful, dads get involved in many activities that gobble up precious time. This brings on great time pressure because Dad is trying to accomplish his responsibilities with less time available than he needs. Is this truly the Lord's will for our time?

These verses tell us the mindset that God wants us to have: "I beseech you therefore, brethren, by the mercies of God, that ye present your bodies a living sacrifice, holy, acceptable unto God, *which is* your reasonable service. And be not conformed to this world: but be ye transformed by the renewing of your mind, that ye may prove what *is* that good, and acceptable, and perfect, will of God" (Romans 12:1-2).

We are bought with the precious blood of Jesus. We have been purchased to be His children and to be used for His glory. As long as we have breath, He has purpose for all of our time for all of our lives. He wants that time used not for our recreation but rather for His kingdom. Galatians 5:13 tells us what our freedom in Christ is for. "For, brethren, ye have been called unto liberty; only *use* not liberty for an occasion to the flesh, but by love serve one another."

Stealing Time?

Consider the following time-robber analogy. Assume for a minute that you have started your own business. You worked hard every available hour to get it going. It cost you some sleep, but you were finally able to leave your corporate job and come home. Then over the weeks, your business grew little by little. You were getting busier and busier, and after a year, you were at the point of needing to hire an employee.

You knew it would be very difficult because you didn't have quite enough money to hire someone, but you desperately needed help. You decided that if you cut back your income, you could hire an employee. You shopped around and finally found someone with the skill set you felt was needed. It was a relief to finally have help.

However, within a week of hiring him, you noticed that he was on the phone with his wife a lot, and therefore he wasn't getting all his work done. You needed his help or you wouldn't have hired him, but he was forever on the telephone. Even after discussing it with him and telling him how you had to take a temporary cut in pay to hire him, he still wouldn't quit "stealing" your time by being on the telephone.

Think how troubled you would be in that situation. He wasn't doing anything overtly wrong, yet you were upset because you were paying for his time, you had work for him to do, and he wasn't doing it.

Now compare that to our relationship with the Father. God didn't merely hire us, but He purchased us with the precious blood of Jesus. We are His possessions! "For ye are bought with a price: therefore glorify God in your body, and in your spirit, which are God's" (1 Corinthians 6:20). If we could only understand how valuable we are to the Lord, and how jealous He is for us. Our time is not our time to do with what we want.

Even if it isn't sinful use of time, it is all His time. That is why James 4:4 is so strong. "Ye adulterers and adulteresses, know ye not that the friendship of the world is enmity with God? whosoever therefore will be a friend of the world is the enemy of God." It is interesting to note that the Greek word for friend is "philos" and means to have a fondness. We aren't even to have a fondness for the things of the world, or we are an enemy of God. That might sound harsh, but when we realize that God purchased us with the blood of Jesus, we can understand how He can be so jealous when we give our time to another.

If It Were to End

Now that God's perspective is clear to us, let's look at time robbers from an objective human point of view. Picture yourself to be forty years old. You have been saved since you were twenty and have three children. You have a sudden heart attack and find yourself in ICU with a myriad of wires and hoses connected to you. Every breath is labored, and just to sit up is exhausting. They have finished with the tests, and the doctor comes in to tell you the results. He says that he believes it is inoperable because there is too much damage to the heart, and all they can do is hope for a heart donor. However, the list of recipients is quite long, and he wonders if your heart will last until a new one is secured.

Laying there with so little hope of extending your life, you think about your wife and children. You married late, and your children are young. There is still much that needs to be done in raising your children in the nurture and admonition of the Lord. Your job has kept you busy, and you just haven't spent the time with the children that you could have. You had hoped to change, but now it's too late. No amount of money can buy more time.

At that moment, the true preciousness of time would be appreciated. Sadly, you had not learned to redeem your time or to number your days. You reflect on the years of watching both the six o'clock and the ten o'clock news each evening. It was only an hour, but an hour a day over the years since your children were born is now priceless. You loved watching games on the weekends, too, but never considered yourself a fanatic. You also enjoyed watching two movies a week, one with the children and one with your wife. You now realize those hours had no eternal benefit at all; they were nothing. Even five minutes of talking on the couch would have been far more beneficial to your relationships with your loved ones than those hours in front of "the tube." Then there were other activities as well on which you wasted time. Now it is too late, and there is no way to redeem the time that was wasted.

Description of a Time Robber

Time robbers are very sneaky fellows. They hide their real identities because otherwise people would not welcome them into their lives and homes. They deceive the innocent and steal their most valuable possession—time.

When I was nine, my dad built a very cool go-cart for me. After about a year of driving it, the novelty had worn off, and at one point, it wouldn't start. I reasoned I didn't need a go-cart that wouldn't run so I traded it to a neighbor boy for a catcher's mitt that I could use. I was clearly taken advantage of because the mitt was nothing in value compared to that go-cart. I was deceived by my "friend."

Dad's time when applied to the lives of the children and God's kingdom is priceless, yet Satan would like to deceive Dad by getting him to trade that time away by spending it on countless, meaningless pursuits.

Time robbers come under many different guises, so I can't give you a mug shot to look at. The best way is to describe them. Be sure to read carefully their descriptions so you can spot them in your life before they steal you blind of your time.

> Clever and smoooooooooth talking—They will quickly size you up and target your weaknesses. They will work hard to convince you your time is being well spent with them, encouraging you to choose what might be considered good versus God's best.

> Freedom versus obedience—Time robbers will emphasize your freedom in Christ and be careful to avoid the subject of our needed obedience to Christ and serving Him.

> Attractive—The best sales people are good looking. Customers are drawn to their good appearance. Time robbers are often visually appealing and might be considered "eye candy."

Very far sighted—If they can't steal all of your time, they will settle for what time you are willing to part with. Think about it. If they can steal just an hour a day, over twenty years that equates to 7,300 hours. An hour a week would add up to 1,040 hours during that twenty-year period. Even if they can steal only a half hour a week, after twenty years that will be 520 hours they have kept you from being with your children. This is the equivalent of a month of time, assuming a normal day of sixteen waking hours. Time robbers are happy to settle for small bits of time because they know they will eventually add up to large amounts.

Feed the flesh versus the spirit—The flesh wants fun, pleasure, and excitement. The Spirit will lead in a path of self-sacrifice and self-denial. Time robbers won't serve others unless there is self-gratification first. They are often whispering in the ears of those who will listen, "Go ahead. You deserve it."

Financially costly—It doesn't make sense that someone should have to pay to be robbed, but it just shows how clever these robbers are. They will convince people to spend large sums of money, to include borrowing from the bank, just to indulge in these time robbers. Internet scams are petty compared to how efficient time robbers are in milking the flock.

Vanity

God's Word sums up time robbers very nicely into the word "vanity." The Hebrew word for "vanity" is *hebel*, and *Vine's Expository Dictionary of Old and New Testament Words* defines it as "breath, vanity, idol." Vanity is like exhaled human breath—a transitory thing, meaningless and purposeless. In essence, a time robber can be summarized as something that takes our time but yields no eternal fruit. It might well be pictured as the exhaled breath that is seen for a moment on a cool day and then quickly fades away.

Here is a picture of God's opinion of vanities:

> "And when the LORD saw *it*, he abhorred *them*, because of the provoking of his sons, and of his daughters. And he said, I will hide my face from them, I will see what their end *shall be*: for they *are* a very froward generation, children in whom *is* no faith. They have moved me to jealousy with *that which is* not God; they have provoked me to anger with their vanities: and I will move them to jealousy with *those which are* not a people; I will provoke them to anger with a foolish nation" (Deuteronomy 32:19-21).

May each dad evaluate how he spends his time. Most will only reject an activity if it is proven sinful, but the reason for rejecting activities should be whether the Father will reap fruit from it. Are we spending our time on things that will bear eternal fruit? "Herein is my Father glorified, that ye bear much fruit; so shall ye be my disciples" (John 15:8). If we are following the Lord, He will direct us in paths of righteousness that will bear the spiritual fruit He desires from our lives.

Specifically

As I shared previously, "nothing becomes dynamic until it becomes specific," and so it is time to name names. I have found that when I like something, even if I know it isn't good for me, it can still be very difficult to part with it. However, when I focus on the damage being done to my family, then I can be moved to action. Please have a heart open to the working of the Spirit and choose to cast out all the vanities of this life that will bear no positive eternal fruit. These time robbers are also great hindrances to your time management. They keep you from redeeming the time and from numbering your days.

I am going to move through time robbers with which I have done battle. In discussing with men their time pressures, it has become clear that these are the majority of time robbers. There are more, of course. If I didn't list yours, I hope your heart will be open to evaluating your time before the Lord and asking Him what those time robbers might be.

TV: The Beast

"I've been praying for eighteen years to throw out the TV or at least the cable and certainly the video game systems. My husband uses electronics to unwind . . . a family walk would sure be nice sometimes. Otherwise he is a wonderful husband. I just am jealous of the electronic mistresses. Sigh."

The beast is one of the worst time robbers. Look at how this dad is trading away his time in front of the TV. He is undermining his relationship with his wife and most likely with his children. Valuable time that he could spend with his family in the Word is being thrown away, and he is probably not keeping up with other responsibilities either.

Not only does TV steal precious time, but it is like a turkey injector. The one I use is a big syringe with a large needle. You fill it up with something flavorful, and then inject it into the turkey's muscle prior to cooking. Injecting the turkey this way gives it a new flavor from the inside out that basting can't achieve. In a similar way, the beast will inject not good, but bad influence into the hearts of the family even though the family finds it tasty. Over time those hearts will be turned toward the love of the world and the evil it has to offer.

Think about it. Why else would the world watch TV if it didn't appeal to them? Most consider it harmless entertainment, but sadly, at the very least it whets the appetite for all the evils the world has to offer. What was considered pornography years ago is broadcast on prime time for general viewing. What about all the supposedly harmless science and nature shows that fill children's minds with humanistic and evolutionistic ideas? The beast is probably the most serious time robber, and Dad is the one God holds accountable for it being in the home. "But whoso shall offend one of these little ones which believe in me, it were better for him that a millstone were hanged about his neck, and *that* he were drowned in the depth of the sea" (Matthew 18:6).

"My husband is a senior pastor. Our life revolves around that in all ways! The only recreational activities we do consistently are watch TV, go out to dinner or a movie, or go to someone's house (someone in the church). My husband is involved in our children's lives but not in the area of leading us in Bible study times."

Here is a dad who has eliminated almost all of the time robbers from his life. Isn't it amazing, though, how we hold onto some things so tightly? This dad is trading away the spiritual leadership of his own children for TV and movies. What if he stopped those two activities? How much time would he gain to spend with his children reading the Word?

Sports

Sports are probably the most addictive time robbers. Slightly tongue in cheek, I feel that many dads would part more quickly with their wives than they would with following or participating in sports. The addiction goes so deep that it can take only the power of the Holy Spirit and a hunger for obedience to the Word to overcome it and set a man free. I have written and taught a fair amount on the subject of sports (see Resources at the back of the book for information on an audio CD called *Sports–Friend or Foe?*) so I won't duplicate it here. For a man who seeks to make the Lord Jesus supreme in his life and be busy about the Lord's things, I wonder if he will have time for sports.

> *"I, the wife, do the yard work. We pay to have the vehicle maintained, and we have many unfinished house duties. Right now our family of four spends about ten hours a week on the baseball fields."*

What could this man do with the ten hours a week that he is now putting in at the baseball fields? He could have a daily, forty-five minute family Bible time and still have 4.75 hours left over for car and home maintenance. He would be leading his family spiritually, keeping up with his home responsibilities, teaching his sons skills, fellowshipping with them, and helping them grow up to a life of productivity rather than being ensnared by the time robber of sports.

Moderate exercise should not be confused with sports. Sports can be highly addictive and a great waste of eternal time, while enough exercise to maintain health is at least a little profitable. "For bodily exercise profiteth little: but godliness is profitable unto all things, having promise of the life that now is, and of that which is to come" (1 Timothy 4:8). As stated earlier, there are great ways to stay fit in far less time than participating in sports. Paul is saying there is some benefit to exercise. Therefore we can seek out those value bucks and use each exercising minute wisely by walking or running with a family member. This avoids being involved in sports for exercise and thus eliminates the possibility of giving our children a passion for the time robber of sports. In addition, our exercise time doubles as fellowship time.

"I wanted to comment on the amount of hours my husband spends in recreational activities. He enjoys exercising, and it helps him relieve the stress of a high-stress job, so he spends a lot of time training for various races/triathlons. He does all of his training early in the morning so it NEVER affects his family time, and we attend all of the races during the 'season' as his cheering section. He has really included us in this, and I am sincerely glad he does it because it really helps keep him healthy and less stressed (he has a lot of heart issues in his family and is trying to take care of himself for us)."

Here we have a dad whose wife supports his choice of time usage for exercise. However, are they making choices with eternal benefits? While this husband gets up early in the morning for his exercising thinking it doesn't impact family time, it really does, because he isn't having family Bible time (this was indicated on the survey response). If he weren't exercising so long, he could leave for work earlier, come home earlier, and have time in the Word with his wife and children in the evening. By being attentive to his health, this dad is blessing his family, but he is likely spending more time than is necessary to achieve a healthy heart. If he cut back on his exercising, he could use those extra hours to spiritually grow his family. In addition, he is using exercise as a stress reliever rather than depending on the Lord Jesus and maturing spiritually to help him deal with stress.

Recreational Hunting and Fishing

Recreational hunting and fishing can fleece many hours and dollars. There may be a few who truly need to provide food on the table by hunting and fishing. I have met one family for which that might be the case. If a person is honest with himself, he will see that the thrill of the hunt, catching the "big one," having time away, or some other reason such as these is what fuels this time robber. There is no doubt, there can be some quality talking time between a father and his son when alone, out fishing somewhere. This is where the false justification comes in to divert Dad's attention from the truth.

Far better would it be for Dad to spend time with his son teaching him a skill by working together in the yard, on the car, or building a deck. These can provide more edifying time together than hunting or fishing would because of the other benefits that come from using our time this way. When we are with our sons on a work project we don't have to be away from our families, we accomplish a task that needs to be done, we save money that would have been spent on the trip, and we don't give our sons an appetite for this time robber of recreational hunting and fishing.

Computer Pastimes

Computer pastimes can be the most dangerous of all. The computer as a tool can be very, very productive, but like a chainsaw, it can be disastrously harmful. If a chainsaw were accidentally applied to a man's arm, that arm would never be the same, no matter how good the surgeon. There must be proper use and protection when operating a chainsaw, and the computer is the same way. The computer that I use is both fully protected and open for Teri's inspection. She receives a report of every Internet site I visit, and I will gladly answer any questions she has about website visits or e-mail correspondence.

"I wish my husband didn't watch basketball or play computer games, and that he spent time in daily devotions and led our family in devotional times more regularly. If this were the case, I really would have no complaints. He is otherwise a wonderful husband."

Look at the heart cry coming from this family. They are yearning for a husband and father who will put a higher priority on feeding them spiritually than he does on satisfying his own wants and desires. How sad to be a wonderful husband in every area, but to fail in this one that has eternal consequences.

We hear stories of dads who waste enormous amounts of time on the computer on an ongoing basis. Some are playing Internet sports or other computer gaming, some reading news, and others just surfing. In addition, many are addicted to pornography and use the Internet to feed this wickedness. Satan goes about as a roaring lion, and man is all too eager to step into his path. "Be sober, be vigilant; because your adversary the devil, as a roaring lion, walketh about, seeking whom he may devour" (1 Peter 5:8). If a computer can't be guarded and used properly, I would plead with you to get rid of it.

Socializing

Even getting together with friends can be a time robber. First, let me state clearly that fellowship, which edifies in the Lord Jesus, is a wonderful gift from the Lord. But notice the qualifier "edifies." I don't believe that fellowship is a time robber, but I do want to consider other social get-togethers that aren't edifying.

I've known families who have a perceived need for getting together with friends that seems out of balance. They exhibit a far greater dependence on others than the Lord Jesus. They get together socially to eat, talk, watch movies, and play games, while the children are off playing by themselves. Later Dad and Mom are shocked to find out their children have been exposed

> *We (I) have to continually work to ensure our fellowship time is purposeful and not just "relaxing together." Am I encouraging them in the Lord? Have I challenged them? Have I asked about their spiritual walk? Am I praying with them? If it's not purposeful, it turns into wasted time.*

to wrong things, and they blame the other families. Who took the children there and didn't want to interrupt the adult time by overseeing the children? Children are going to be children, and that is why God holds the parents accountable. The major reason these activities aren't edifying is that the families don't have Bible time and a time of worship together because that isn't as much fun as eating and talking.

Real fellowshipping is edifying for all involved, parents and children. A building project in the physical realm takes effort. In the same way, to make socializing time profitable, someone will have to make sure that all the children are supervised and that Bible time happens. Soon families will not only come to expect edification, but they will also see that it is what makes fellowship even sweeter.

Big Boy Toys and Activities

Big boy toys and activities are often the most costly time robbers. The list seems limitless: motorboats, sailboats, motorcycles, four-wheelers, jet skis, airplanes, skydiving, hang gliding, mountain climbing, canoeing, kayaking, and recreational vehicles. There are still more that I didn't list.

When we lived in Florida, I was bitten by the "boat bug." I'm sure it wasn't my fault because I caught it from those I was working with. It must have been very infectious because several of the guys at work had boats. The talk was often about their boats and what they were going to do over the weekend. It was only a matter of time before I was bitten and would want to spend several thousand dollars for a "bathtub with a sail" on it. Harry was the main one encouraging me, and he even helped me find a place where we could "park" my boat. I knew it was painful to the family finances, but I didn't give a thought to the far greater impact it was having on our family time since we couldn't all go sailing together. My passion became time on my sailboat. If you would have asked me if my love for my Lord was diminished by my love for sailing, I would have said, "Of course not!!!" Yet I was squandering every minute I had available on my new boat.

Understand, I judge no man, but here is the great challenge with this time robber. As with computers, someone may own something in the list above and use it as a tool and not a toy. However, to use it as a tool, careful attention must be paid so that it doesn't become a toy and a time robber. In addition, we can easily give our children an appetite for these time robbers if we do not remain on guard.

We currently have what is titled as an RV. It is, however, our converted home away from home that we use when giving conferences. I was unable to find anything else that was big enough to transport nine people, a myriad of instruments, sound equipment, and books. We slowly converted this vehicle from a Greyhound bus into our motor home over the course of two years while we traveled in it. The challenge for me is to make sure that I keep using it as only a tool.

Selfish Relaxation

Often as I share these challenges and concepts with men, I hear these kinds of responses. "I am under such pressure all the time at work. I just need to relax by watching TV or playing computer games. This is my outlet, and I deserve it." Here is just such an example:

"My husband is a very hard worker and wonderful provider. My concerns would be in the area of spiritual leadership of

me and the children. When he is home and has down time,
he tends to 'waste it' on watching TV to relax. The children
will watch it with him, but it just seems like a waste of an
evening. I've brought up the schedule, but he doesn't seem to
be interested. I don't feel like we have a spiritual vision for
our family."

First, let me assure you that needing to relax in this way is
a lie Satan has used well to justify time robbers. If we have an
excuse for letting our time go to time robbers, we feel no need
for change. We are satisfied with feeding our flesh with the little
time we have available rather than investing it in pursuits with
eternal value.

From personal experience, I have discovered that I can
relax as I eat dinner with my family and as I spend time in the
Word with them. I am then re-ener-
gized for the more rigorous activities
in my evening. I want to challenge
you to consider the potential in your
life that will come if you can let go
of the idea that selfish relaxation
pursuits are necessary. Use your
family dinners and time in the Word
for relaxation and your Sundays as a day of rest.

This issue reminds me of
the time of the Judges:
Everyone did what was
right in their own eyes.
What is right in our
eyes may be an affront
to God. Stay in the
Word!

The Hidden Cost

Remember how clever time robbers are? They will convince dads of reasons why a time robber is really a dear friend.
One of the best ways they do this is to justify some good that
"could" come by it. I can't remember for sure, but I wouldn't be
a bit surprised if I justified my sailboat to Teri by saying it
would be a way to spend more time with the children. The
reality is that it was something that I could do with a child or
two, but not the whole family. In addition, by focusing on a

perceived good that would result, one neglects looking for an even better use of time.

I had failed to see another fruit of time robbers: I was setting my children up to embrace sailing as wholeheartedly as I had. I was potentially giving them my passion for sailing. As adults, they might have chosen to spend their time pursuing the same worthless time robber rather than being productive for the Lord. Now that is a real prize to a time robber. He bags two or more people's time with the same effort.

Radical Time Management

I want you to think with me for a minute about the time robbers you have in your life. Mentally add up the amount of time they are currently taking from your week. Now consider where you are facing time pressure and how much time you would need to be free of that pressure. If you were to give up your time robbers, would you gain the time to accomplish those tasks you should be doing but aren't finding the time to do? This is simply the easiest, but most profound, time management secret that you have at your disposal. By avoiding time robbers, you will gain a significant amount of time to tackle those tasks you are not getting to and those that are putting time pressure in your life.

I understand feelings of great reluctance to let go of certain time robbers, so I want to encourage you with my personal experience. Every time robber that I have listed is one which I have, with the Lord's help, been able to release from my life. Not one of them would I choose to take back. I am so blessed by what I am able to do with my time now that I am free of those despicable time robbers that I not only never want to see them again, but I also would like to see you leave them behind as well. I can only imagine the value to God's kingdom if every

Christian man would eliminate the time robbers from his life in order to use his time to obediently serve the Lord Jesus Christ.

The Abundant Life

Without much thought, we can see how our country has plunged from being a Christian nation under God to a godless one. Believers have chosen to pursue a time-robbing life of fun and entertainment instead of being instruments of righteousness in the hands of Almighty God. Can you see that when things so "innocent" are left unchecked, they bear bad fruit in a few short years? We are a nation of lovers of pleasures more than lovers of God: "Traitors, heady, highminded, lovers of pleasures more than lovers of God" (2 Timothy 3:4).

That is why God is calling courageous dads, who are willing to forsake these time robbers, to be used of Him for His glory. "Then said Jesus unto his disciples, If any *man* will come after me, let him deny himself, and take up his cross, and follow me" (Matthew 16:24). It will cost you, but oh, the joy unspeakable that awaits. We are the Lord's servants, and if we spend His time as He directs, we will have the abundant life that He gives. "The thief cometh not, but for to steal, and to kill, and to destroy: I am come that they might have life, and that they might have *it* more abundantly" (John 10:10). You can lose the time robbers in exchange for a life of time management without time pressure. You will be redeeming your time and numbering your days. A joyful life is far superior to a fun-filled one.

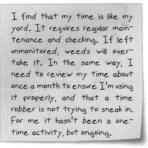

I find that my time is like my yard. It requires regular maintenance and checking. If left unmonitored, weeds will overtake it. In the same way, I need to review my time about once a month to ensure I'm using it properly, and that a time robber is not trying to sneak in. For me it hasn't been a one-time activity, but ongoing.

The Schedule

An important tool I want to address in our time-management discussion is the use of a schedule. Many will resist making a schedule because they don't want to be bound by a plan, or they think they couldn't possibly schedule because their days are too hectic. However, I have found the benefits of a schedule outweigh its disadvantages, so I will offer information about a schedule and encourage you to set aside any negative predispositions. There is a decision that must take place: we must choose to either live with time pressures and robbers or to invest the effort needed to manage our time and eliminate the robbers. Both take energy, but there will be peace and productivity if we choose to manage our time.

Biblical Basis

Let's begin by evaluating whether there is a biblical basis for using a schedule. Here are verses that have to do with time and order.

> "So teach *us* to number our days, that we may apply *our* hearts unto wisdom" (Psalms 90:12).

> "Redeeming the time, because the days are evil" (Ephesians 5:16).

"Walk in wisdom toward them that are without, redeeming the time" (Colossians 4:5).

"To every *thing there is* a season, and a time to every purpose under the heaven" (Ecclesiastes 3:1).

"Let all things be done decently and in order" (1 Corinthians 14:40).

"For though I be absent in the flesh, yet am I with you in the spirit, joying and beholding your order, and the stedfastness of your faith in Christ" (Colossians 2:5).

Obviously, we don't find the word *schedule* in these verses. However, as you endeavor to bring order to your life through your purposeful time management, I want you to consider that a schedule could be a beneficial tool to help you toward success. God has determined set times for His creation: days and nights, seasons, the life cycles of plants and animals—they all run on the schedule God made for them. We, too, can choose to use a schedule to help us accomplish what God has called us to do.

There is another benefit to having one's life in order. "And when the queen of Sheba had seen all Solomon's wisdom, and the house that he had built, And the meat of his table, and the sitting of his servants, and the attendance of his ministers, and their apparel, and his cupbearers, and his ascent by which he went up unto the house of the LORD; there was no more spirit in her" (1 Kings 10:4-5). The queen of Sheba was an unbeliever who blessed the name of the Lord for all she saw in Solomon's household—its order, the way it was run, and the joy in the home. She was moved to say, "Blessed be the LORD thy God, which delighted in thee, to set thee on the throne of Israel: because the LORD loved Israel for ever, therefore made he thee king, to do judgment and justice" (1 Kings 10:9). Don't you desire that when unbelievers are near your family or in your home, they come away praising God for His goodness and mercy that is lived out in your home? A schedule is an important aspect of bringing God glory through transforming chaos and pressure into order and peace.

What Is a Schedule?

A schedule is nothing more than a budget for your time. Most men are familiar with how financial budgets help a family live within their financial means, allow them to maximize each paycheck, and enable them to save for future expenditures. A schedule will have similar benefits for time. It will be a reality check for which activities and projects can fit into your available time and which things should be rejected. A schedule helps you to be the most productive with your hours, and it lets you use time little by little to accomplish what normally would take large chunks of time.

> With a schedule you find that things are less of a surprise and deadlines do not sneak up on you.

When you have a schedule in place, your time is directed by that schedule. You don't have to continually make decisions as to what you are going to do and when you are going to do it. You have a plan already put in place, and all you have to do is choose to follow it. You won't be wasting time trying to decide what to do next or simply doing nothing because you can't figure it out. A schedule lets us be purposeful with our time so that we don't come to the end of an evening or day off frustrated because we have nothing to show for those hours. Your schedule can be a tool to help you eliminate time robbers because you will likely gravitate to them when you don't have a plan for utilizing your time in beneficial ways.

Is It Even Possible?

One of the greatest challenges a dad faces in being receptive to scheduling is right behind his eyes. He often believes that the demands on his time are fluid, and nothing as rigid as a schedule could possibly work. That is what moms have thought as well, but our first book, *Managers of Their Homes*, was written to help homeschooling moms develop and use a schedule. These moms have shared with us their stories of success. We have, in our basement, boxes filled with thousands upon thousands of testimonies from moms who have stated how a schedule has brought them peace and productivity out of pressure and chaos. If a schedule works for busy, homeschooling moms, it will work for dads too.

Maybe you might be tempted to think that a dad's time demands are far different from a stay-at-home mom's. A dad goes to work and has little time at home. When he gets home, he finds many people clamoring for his time.

All the more reason for a schedule since time is so limited.

Let's compare that to Mom. She doesn't go away to work, but her time has many demands upon it—housework, meals, exercise, personal time in the Word, childcare, being a helpmeet to her husband, ministry, and perhaps homeschooling. One would look at a list like that and wonder if a mom could ever schedule such a diversity of tasks with such variability to them.

Honestly, this is what makes a schedule valuable. The less we have, the more we need to budget it (time, money, etc).

Children's needs cause many difficulties to a schedule because they are often unschedulable. Then there is the fact that Mom's work is 24/7.

It's true that when Dad comes home from work, there may be a line waiting to pounce on him asking for his time. But what about Mom? Doesn't she have the same number in line making demands on her time? Dad himself is usually in the queue, making requests on Mom's time before he leaves for work, over the phone while he is at work, or when he arrives home. Often the things that Dad doesn't get to, he asks Mom to do. Mom actually has a more difficult time adhering to a schedule than Dad does. Since we know firsthand that stay-at-home moms can successfully schedule, we want to encourage you that any dad who chooses to schedule can do so.

Mom's scheduling is so complex because she is scheduling for herself and the children. Therefore, we found it was important to have a Scheduling Kit included with the scheduling book we wrote for moms. Since Dad just needs a schedule for his own at-home hours, the tools of a kit aren't necessary. Scheduling a dad's time is far easier than a mom's.

What about Being Spirit-led?

We have sometimes heard objections to scheduling from those who say they don't want to use a schedule because they want to be Spirit-led. To be perfectly honest with you, when I hear this, I usually wonder if it is an excuse used by those who don't want to exercise self-discipline or accountability for their time.

When we make a schedule, the main goal of that schedule is to use our time in obedience to the Lord Jesus Christ. That will only happen as we seek Him and follow the Spirit's leading for setting up our schedules. Therefore, the schedule itself is helping us to be Spirit-led—to be consistent in following the Lord's direction for our time and our lives.

There will also be times when the Spirit chooses to alter our schedule. At these moments, it is evident that there is a reason to depart from the schedule for an hour, an evening, or even a more extended period of time. For example, I can remember a couple of nights when I came home from work to find Teri in tears from a discouraging, exhausting day with the children. I took her in my arms, gave her a kiss, and asked if she would like to go out for a date. I wish you could have seen the transformation in her face! Dinner was already prepared, so we left the older children in charge of the younger ones to eat and clean up. Teri and I went out to eat, and of course, we talked the whole time. We were home for family Bible time and putting the children to bed. I missed several parts of my evening schedule, but Teri felt loved and encouraged. That was a Spirit-led change in the evening schedule.

"Be careful for nothing; but in every thing by prayer and supplication with thanksgiving let your requests be made known unto God. And the peace of God, which passeth all understanding, shall keep your hearts and minds through Christ Jesus" (Philippians 4:6-7). Because a schedule helps a man accomplish what the Lord Jesus has called him to do, it plays an important part in helping him not feel anxious and have a peaceful heart.

Your Wife

Seek your wife's counsel as you begin designing your schedule. She knows you better than anyone else and is aware of the demands on your time. She might have suggestions about what needs to be accomplished and whether your schedule is workable. What you schedule for the hours you are at home will affect both her and the children.

You will want your wife's input when you are working on your schedule because the two of you, as a team, will be managing any activities that involve the children. She will be key in figuring out how long an activity such as dinner cleanup will take, what the children need to do in the evening that affects the schedule, and when they should go to bed. Having your wife's counsel during the design stage of your schedule will help when you start following the schedule because she will be "on board." Once you begin to implement the schedule, she may have suggestions as to how to tweak it to make it more efficient.

The more hours you are home during the day, the more important it is that you work with your wife in making up a schedule for you, for her, and for the children. Once again, the team concept comes into play, and the two of you must put together the schedules based on the various needs of the family. Sometimes this might mean that you have to do an activity in the evening that you would prefer to do in the morning. It could mean that your wife gets up earlier in the morning than she would like to get up. However, with prayer and coopera- tion, I believe you will be pleasantly surprised at what a schedule can do for your whole family.

It may also be possible that you will have to help your wife become more time organized and efficient when you begin using a schedule, especially if she is somewhat challenged in these areas. If you schedule dinner at a particular time after you have arrived home from work, that part of the schedule is dependent on your wife having dinner ready to eat at the scheduled time. If Mom does not use a schedule for her time, it will be quite difficult to have dinner ready to eat when you have mealtime on your schedule.

In this case, I would recommend that you discuss with your wife when to begin dinner preparations every night so that it is ready at the designated mealtime. You wife might be ben- efitted and blessed if you purchase *Managers of Their Homes* for her so that she can learn how to make and use a schedule.

Evenings with Activities

What would one do with their scheduling when they are home every weeknight except for one? This is a common scenario with Christian families who are involved in churches that have Wednesday evening services. In this case, you just drop your normal evening activities after dinner and replace them with church. It is likely that the children's bedtime, and perhaps yours as well, will be later on this night after fitting in family Bible time either before or after church. You could plan for family Bible to be shorter than normal, but I would encourage you not to skip it even though you will be at church that evening.

There will be occasional other evenings when you will release your usual schedule. Our family often invites guests over for dinner on Friday evenings. That means we eat, talk, and have family Bible time with our company—Christians and non-Christians. All the other aspects of my schedule are set aside for that night.

I would encourage you to be cautious about how often you commit your family to evening activities, especially if your family has Wednesday night church. It becomes exhausting for a family to be continually away from home at night, getting to bed late. In addition, when you are away from home frequently, you can't keep up with your scheduled activities. Occasionally this won't matter, but on a regular basis you will definitely notice the effects. You will soon find yourself back to the time struggles and pressures that you are wanting to leave behind.

The Fifteen- and Thirty-Minute Gold Mine

Often we think we need an hour, two hours, or more to tackle a project. This might be true of something like painting, which will take quite a bit of preparation before the project can begin and cleanup before you can leave it. However, you would be amazed at what a gold mine a thirty-minute block of time can be. Put thirty minutes in your evening schedule for household projects, and then look at your project list. Spend thirty minutes on the top priority on the list. The first thirty minutes, you might only get the tools collected up that you need. However, that is a start. By the end of a week of utilizing your thirty-minute time blocks, you could be quite surprised at what you have accomplished. Track that thirty-minute part of your schedule for a month to see what it has netted for you. Multiply it over the course of your lifetime, and you will realize what a gold mine being diligent for thirty minutes each day can be for your time management.

This is also true for fifteen minutes a day. Perhaps you have had a desire to memorize Scripture, but you never get around to it. Put it on your schedule for fifteen minutes. Maybe you want to read Christian biographies out loud to your children. Schedule that for fifteen minutes each evening. It could be that you are never caught up with the record keeping for your finances. Tackle it for fifteen minutes every night.

You will be pleasantly amazed at how much you accomplish and what you have to show for your at-home weekday hours when you use a schedule. Until one begins to utilize a schedule, they usually aren't aware of the amount of time that is wasted on time robbers, indecision, and lack of direction.

Tweaking Your Schedule

Once you have a schedule put together and begin implementing it, you may have to tweak it. I would suggest that you use it for at least two weeks before you make any revisions because it is going to take several days for you and your family to become accustomed to following the schedule. The first day of a schedule, it may appear that you haven't allowed enough time for a particular activity, when in reality it just took the family some time to move into the activity and get going with it. For example, you call the family for Bible time. Several children immediately head for the bathroom, delaying their arrival in the living room by five minutes. Then two of them discover they don't have their Bibles so they take off looking for them, only to return another five minutes later. The phone rings as you start explaining to your family how you want to have family Bible time. Your wife answers the phone. Even though she is trying to end the conversation quickly, it takes her five minutes to do so.

You have now lost fifteen of the thirty minutes you had scheduled for family Bible. Don't be discouraged, and don't change the schedule. Recognize that a schedule will ferret out character deficiencies in your children and yourself. Don't react to it, but embrace it as an opportunity to seek out those problems and raise responsible children. Begin to train your children to recognize when Bible time is to occur so that they will go to the bathroom and find their Bibles beforehand. Have older children collect younger siblings who can't tell time, and bring them to the living room. Learn not to answer the phone during your Bible reading or have one person designated to answer it, tell the caller you are having Bible time, and take a message.

On the first night of your schedule, you might have been discouraged by all the time that was missing from Bible time by distractions. However, I believe that within a few short days, you will have ironed out those wrinkles and be excitedly utilizing your family Bible time.

After two weeks on a schedule, if there are still areas that aren't working well, tweak the schedule. Perhaps you have scheduled fifteen minutes for dinner cleanup, but you find that every night the cleanup takes at least twenty minutes and sometimes twenty-five. At that point, you should either modify the schedule to allow for more cleanup time or assign additional cleanup helpers to bring the task back into the boundaries of the scheduled time.

In a Not-So-Perfect World

What about the dad who says, "I can't schedule because I get off work at different times every day"? Remember how I began the scheduling discussion with the statement that the greatest hindrance to scheduling is right behind a man's eyes? I believe you will find that if a dad has the attitude that he is committed to making a schedule work so that he can be a good steward of his time before his God, it will work.

The first step is to make sure this dad is being honest with himself. I've observed men through the years who could have left work at a consistent time. However, they were either undisciplined in their work and had to work later, or they were consumed by their job and unwilling to stop for the day. I have known other dads whose work departure time was truly beyond their control, and that time varied greatly. If a dad can make it home consistently, he needs to. If he can't, there are some things that can be done.

One thing a dad could do is ask that his wife plan dinner nightly for a later time. On Dad's schedule, he would shift his discretionary time blocks so that they fall prior to dinner. Mom should adjust lunch so that the children are not all waiting around starving until the dinner time arrives. It would mean that Dad forgoes his personal projects on days that he comes home late. On those days, he may have to walk in and sit down to eat without even changing clothes. After dinner cleanup, family Bible time and praying with the children would be scheduled before they needed to get to bed. Can you see how a schedule facilitates even crazy work hours?

I believe this approach will work with military dads. As long as dinner is scheduled as late as possible, there can be time with Dad prior to the children's bedtime. It might even mean that the children's bedtimes are moved later to accommodate Dad's return home. One of the blessings of home education is that the children's whole schedule can be slid later to accommodate time with Dad. They may then be getting up later or using naps to make up for lost nighttime sleep and having a normal school day with Mom. Once Dad wants to make a schedule work, it will work.

Even an OTR Truck Driver

There are some jobs that make it very difficult to schedule Dad's time. I think that an over-the-road truck driver's life would be one of the worst. I've met some single men who are truckers, and they don't even have a home because they are gone all the time. The first question to consider is whether trucking is the Lord's will for Dad's vocation. If Dad isn't home enough to disciple the children, and he is merely bringing home a paycheck, is he fulfilling his greatest calling? What is enough time at home for discipleship of the children? Only the Lord, Dad, and Mom can answer that question through much prayer and discussion.

Assuming Dad is home at least a couple days a week, then it is critical to schedule those days. Throughout Dad's days at home, the family would be included in all of his activities. Each minute becomes priceless, and additional family Bible time would be reasonable. Individual meetings with the children would be very important, along with as much talking time with Mom as possible. A schedule is key to an OTR truck driver raising his children in the nurture and admonition of the Lord.

Schedule Flexibility, Creativity, and Interruptions

Sometimes life circumstances require one to have creativity in making up a schedule. Pray, asking the Lord for His help. One of the men who was a test reader and scheduler for this book works on-call from his home. There was never a certain time that he could schedule family Bible time and know that he would be available. The solution we came up with for family Bible time was to schedule it for two different times, one earlier in the day and one after supper. That way, if he missed it at one time because he'd been called away, he should be able to make it the other time.

Let's say one day he misses the earlier family Bible time and knows he will be out on call at supper time. He could choose to bump family Bible time to one of his personal project times. His wife and children will likely have other activities that are on their schedules that they would be planning to do at that time. In this case, the wife needs to postpone the activities she will be missing and do them at the normally scheduled family Bible time after supper, which is now open.

Whenever there is an interruption to your schedule, the schedule actually helps you deal with that interruption. As you become familiar with your schedule, you will know what activities are the most expendable and can be dropped from the schedule. You will also know what activities could be postponed until a later time in the day, accomplished earlier in the day, or shortened to allow for the interruption. For example, the evening I am writing this section, we have a funeral to attend at 7:00, the time we are normally right in the middle of family Bible. Tonight, we will eat dinner a half hour early, go to the funeral, and have family Bible time when we get home. That means we won't have music time, nor will I have my normal evening computer time.

The List

One key to managing your time is knowing what you will do when you have available time. For most time slots, what you will do is self-evident. When the alarm clock goes off, you get up. When it is dinnertime, you eat, and at family Bible time, you read the Bible. However, when you have time for projects, what do you do? If you don't have a plan for your project time, you will gravitate to time robbers or simply doing nothing. Then projects pile up, producing even more time pressure. To know what you should do when that project time is available, it is important to keep a running "to do" list. Be prepared that it will take effort to organize your time and be efficient with it. Anything of value takes effort.

There are basically two types of projects that will require Dad's attention: recurring and one-time. One-time jobs would be those such as painting the house or fixing a broken door handle, while those that must be done on a recurring basis would be ones such as mowing the lawn or changing the car's oil.

Recurring Jobs

Recurring tasks by definition happen on a regular basis and are pretty easy to schedule. If we make a list of them, we will accomplish them and relieve the mental pressure of trying to keep them in our minds.

Years ago I hired a national lawn service company to fertilize our lawn and kill the weeds. I hired them because I was bothered by the feeling of needing to do something for the lawn, but I didn't think I had the time to do it myself, nor did I know what to do. I stayed with them for some period of time because they were inexpensive. However, the results were terrible. I would call the lawn service to come out and discuss why the yard didn't look good, and they inevitably told me that we'd had too much rain, too little water, or some other reason. They would re-treat the yard at no cost, but it still didn't look good.

I finally thought that surely lawn maintenance isn't rocket science, and that I could learn what to put down and at what time it should be applied. I found there are a host of websites that will tell you when to use certain chemicals for lawn maintenance, and in which regions of the country. I began following those suggestions. Suddenly, my yard looked green, healthy, and weed free for the first time for the same amount of money as I had been spending for the lawn service. I used the calendar feature of Outlook (iCal for Apple users), the office management software I use on my computer, to remind me that it was time to make those applications, and there was one less "worry" with which I had to deal.

Now that my son Jesse is old enough, I'm training him to take over all the yard responsibilities. He mows and trims as needed, and he feeds and weeds when I tell him to. The next step will be to teach him to fully manage that aspect so he knows when he must treat the yard. The time that it takes to teach Jesse are value bucks in action and will pay yearly dividends for my time. Scheduling recurring tasks greatly simplifies our lives, eliminating pressure.

There are many other tasks that can be recurring, such as:

Car maintenance needs

Changing out home HVAC filters

Changing water filters

Giving haircuts

Cutting and splitting wood

Buying anniversary, birthday, and Christmas presents for one's wife

Ministry outings such as nursing homes, distributing tracts, and visiting homeless shelters

One-Time Projects

Probably the majority of items on a to-do list will be one-time projects. Their urgency and priority on the list is usually determined by the level of need, inconvenience, or damage that is being caused until it is taken care of.

Right now the top items I have on my one-time task list are:

Fix our bathroom vanity cold water faucet

Fix the lower track of the girls' shower door

Put up French-door blinds

Organize keys

Troubleshoot outlet upstairs

Often one project will take up all of a particular scheduled project time. You might be able to finish it in that amount of time, but don't discount working on a one-time project for a scheduled block of time, not completing the task, and finishing it in the next scheduled project time. It is also possible that you could fit several less time-intensive jobs into one project block of time.

Project-List Tracking

It is important that you find a way to keep track of what needs to be done, but it doesn't matter how you do it. I encourage you to be determined to persevere until you have a method that works for you.

There is the old-fashioned paper-and-pencil approach. Simply get a tablet and write down the things that need to be done. As you finish each task, cross it off. It is very rewarding to see progress being made in keeping up with your responsibilities. With this method, you will have to be creative to get your recurring tasks on your list. You might try using a legal-sized tablet, labeling one page for each month, and putting recurring jobs on the month where they would need to be done. For example, Teri's birthday is in August, so I would want to be praying about and looking for a present in July. Therefore, on July's page, I would write in, "Birthday present for Teri." I like to check the HVAC filters monthly, so I would write that on every page. For those of you who use your computer to help you track your "to do" list, I am sure you can already see the advantages of your method. Paper-and-pencil guys might want to consider switching to the computer. I will explain how the computer saves you time making and keeping your project list in the section below.

Consider keeping your project list handy to the family so they could add new items to it when they become aware of a need. If your list is on the computer, put a paper where family members could write necessary tasks down for you to transfer to your computer. Let me give you a word of caution, though. If your wife puts a job on the list, and you do other tasks from the list but not hers, she will probably be discouraged. I can testify to this from personal experience.

We have a "Jimmy's List" and "Lynn's List."

Using Your Computer or Smart Phone

Computers are an even easier way to manage tasks. The simplest way is to use Outlook or another calendar program. There are even free calendar programs available via the Internet. You can use the "task" feature to enter both your one-time and recurring tasks for a specific day and time. When entering a recurring job, the program will let you tell it how often the job is to be done—perhaps once a week or once a month—from the multiple options available. Then it automatically puts the job on the calendar for those future dates. If you tell the program to remind you that a job is coming up, it will alert you when it is time to do your project. For some projects, I set the reminder to begin reminding me a week or several days in advance. That gives me time to collect the necessary supplies and be prepared when the actual day for the project arrives.

Using the computer for recurring jobs saves time since you don't have to write down each time the task is to occur. In addition, you don't have to get out your calendar to figure out when it should happen next. The computer does all that for you.

One-time jobs can also be listed using the "task" feature but without scheduling them for a particular day. Just put the projects on the list and check them off when they are completed. Then the list looks much like a paper-and-pencil list would look, except it is on the computer. Anything that takes time and preparation is good to get entered into the computer calendar with a reminder.

> I use Outlook for recurring tasks, but a pocket day-timer for one-time (always with me). I try to update a seasonal project list so the family can see and review projects and add.

I have been using a smart phone to keep track of both my one-time projects and recurring tasks. Since it is always with me, I can add new items anytime I become aware of a need.

> Most also sync with Outlook.

It doesn't matter how you choose to do it; the important thing is that you have it "written" down somewhere. As long as you are attentive to your list or computer calendar and address the projects when they come up, you will be productive, keep up with your projects, and not be anxious about what isn't yet accomplished.

Put the Tool to Use

A schedule is a God-given tool to help you manage your time to keep up with the responsibilities the Lord Jesus has placed in your life. It helps us in redeeming the time and numbering our days. Knowing exactly what you will do at a certain time eliminates the wasted time involved in making hour-by-hour decisions concerning time usage, and it also ends time that is frittered away doing nothing because a decision isn't made. Putting together a schedule becomes a reality check for the time that is available and how it can be allocated in the time budget. A schedule makes it very clear when time robbers are consuming the prime at-home hours.

Even if you think you could never be bound by a schedule, I want to encourage you to give it a try. Make a realistic schedule for your evenings and days off. Then use that schedule for several weeks. Choose to give it a solid try, and then evaluate the benefits you have realized. It is amazing the difference we can feel emotionally when we are accomplishing what God has called us to do. Rather than feeling stressed, tired, and discouraged, we can feel peaceful, content, and fulfilled. I believe that after your schedule trial, you will be sold.

14

Scheduling Step by Step

In this chapter, I want to give you specific directions for setting up a schedule, along with examples. You will find several other sample schedules in the appendix from dads who have used this material to make and use a schedule. Here, though, I will be discussing various aspects of the sample schedules and why they were put together as they were.

This book has had a major emphasis on encouraging you that your time is His time. Therefore, designing a schedule begins with seeking the Lord in prayer as to how He wants to use your time and the order in which He wants the activities accomplished.

As you pray, write down the activities in which you believe the Lord would have you invest your time based on the vision He has put in your heart for your life and your family's lives. List each activity and a reasonable amount of time for it. Make sure that you have considered your time robbers, and that they are not a part of your list. This information will be helpful to you as you pray about a schedule.

Sample Daily Activity List

Morning

Personal time in the Word and prayer	35 minutes
Exercise	30 minutes
Get ready for work	25 minutes
Breakfast	15 minutes
Commute to work	30 minutes
Before work total	**2 hrs., 20 min.**

Midday

Work and lunch	**9 hours**

Evening

Commute home from work	30 minutes
Dinner	30 minutes
Family Bible time	45 minutes
E-mail	15 minutes
Time with family	60 minutes
Pray with children	15 minutes
Ready for bed/Pray with Wife	30 minutes
Evening total	**3 3/4 hours**
Sleep	**7 1/2 hours**

Sample Weekly Activity List

Sunday School lesson preparation	60 minutes
Errands	120 minutes
Lawn mowing	45 minutes
Phone call with your mother	30 minutes
Date with Wife	90 minutes
Work on finances	30 minutes

Rough Schedule

Next, you will want to establish a rough schedule for the week. Fill in the activities that are priorities and any set times they must occur. List activities earliest to latest and leave gaps where there are no time-specific activities. Try to keep the schedule the same for every day. The more your schedule varies from day to day, the more difficult it will be to learn and be consistent using it. That doesn't mean a schedule would be impossible for you, it simply means it will be more challenging. If you can't use just one general schedule, then try to limit it to two. Remember: the fewer different schedules you have, the better.

What if your activities add up to be more than the time you have available? Take them to the Lord and ask Him to show you which activities to weed out or which ones you can cut down on how often you do them. He won't give you more than you can accomplish in a given day.

Sample Rough Schedule

Wake up and prepare for run	5:30-5:45 a.m.
Personal time in the Word and prayer	5:45-6:20
Run	6:20-6:50
Get ready for work	6:50-7:15
Breakfast	7:15-7:30
Commute to work	7:30-8:00
Work	8:00-5:00 p.m.
Commute home	5:00-5:30
Greet family and change clothes	5:30-5:45
Dinner and cleanup	5:45-6:30
Family Bible time	6:30-7:15
Time with family	7:15-8:15
Pray with children	8:15-8:30
Open	8:30-9:30
Get ready for bed/Pray with Wife	9:30-10:00
Bedtime	10:00

Daily Schedule

Now look over your rough schedule for open times where you could fill in activities that haven't been scheduled yet. There is an hour available between 8:30 and 9:30 p.m. that normally might be stolen by time robbers that could now be productive. You decide that you will use fifteen minutes for e-mail and then mix in other items during different days of the week. You have wanted to spend more time with your wife and will head for bed at 9:15 so you can have time to talk with her.

To make the best use of those remaining open thirty minutes, you will rotate activities for each day of the week. On Mondays you will call your mom. Tuesdays will be your night for finances. Wednesdays you will take thirty minutes to plan Saturday's projects and make sure you have any needed supplies. Thursdays will be used for projects. Fridays and Saturdays will be used to prepare your Sunday School lesson. Sunday will be personal reading time. Are you encouraged that it is possible to get it all done?

Sample Filled-In Evening Schedule

Commute home	5:00-5:30 p.m.
Greet family and change clothes	5:30-5:45
Dinner and cleanup	5:45-6:30
Family Bible time	6:30-7:15
Time with family	7:15-8:15
Pray with children	8:15-8:30
E-mail	8:30-8:45
M/Call Mom; T/Finances; W/Plan project; TH/Project; Fri&Sat/Prepare lesson; Sun/Personal reading	8:45-9:15
Get ready for bed/Pray with Wife	9:15-10:00
Bedtime	10:00 p.m.

Saturdays and Days Off

For Saturdays and other days off, I would suggest having one schedule that you can slightly modify to accommodate large projects or smaller, more routine ones. In essence you will take your normal workday schedule and just vary what you do during your usual commute and work hours. Remember that a productive Saturday schedule starts by getting up in the morning at your normal time so that you maximize your awake hours.

Saturdays could be scheduled like this if you have a remodeling project that requires many work hours.

Saturday Schedule with Variation for Larger Projects

Wake up and prepare for run	5:30-5:45 a.m.
Personal time in the Word and prayer	5:45-6:20
Run	6:20-6:50
Get ready for the day	6:50-7:15
Breakfast	7:15-7:30
Remodeling project	7:30-12:00 p.m.
Lunch	12:00-12:30
Remodeling project	12:30-5:45 p.m.
Dinner and cleanup	5:45-6:30
Family Bible time	6:30-7:15
Time with family	7:15-8:15
Pray with children	8:15-8:30
E-mail	8:30-8:45
Prepare Sunday lesson	8:45-9:15
Get ready for bed/Pray with Wife	9:30-10:00
Bedtime	10:00 p.m.

That is a very simple schedule, and it allows you to make the most efficient use of all of those hours compacted together. If that project was to go on for very long, you would fall behind in other responsibilities. What might a more normal Saturday schedule look like?

Saturday Schedule with Variation for Smaller Projects

Wake up and prepare for run	5:30-5:45 a.m.
Personal time in the Word and prayer	5:45-6:20
Run	6:20-6:50
Get ready for the day	6:50-7:15
Breakfast	7:15-7:30
Time block 1	7:30-12:00 p.m.
Lunch	12:00-12:30
Time block 2	12:30-3:00
Time block 3	3:00-5:45
Dinner and cleanup	5:45-6:30
Family Bible time	6:30-7:15
Time with family	7:15-8:15
Pray with children	8:15-8:30
E-mail	8:30-8:45
Prepare Sunday lesson	8:45-9:15
Get ready for bed/Talk to and pray with Wife	9:30-10:00
Bedtime	10:00 p.m.

Time block 1 could be devoted to house, car, or lawn maintenance. Maintenance is easily put off, and when that happens, it generally grows in proportion to what needs to be accomplished. When you have maintenance on the schedule each week, you will be relieved at how well you are keeping up with those projects. During time block 2, you could tackle what is next on your project list, and time block 3 might be for a family activity.

This sort of structure for the Saturday schedule provides flexibility for various events. Afternoons could be set aside for family activities, family ministry, Dad and Mom dates, errands and grocery shopping, or whatever is on your list of needed projects.

If your weekday evenings are not allowing you time to keep up with your personal projects, you may have to schedule time on Saturdays for doing finances, catching up on e-mail, completing research for future projects, time with the children, or ministry or ministry preparations. If you have a family ministry that is once a month on a Saturday, you can develop a schedule for that particular Saturday that takes into consideration the time involved in the ministry and that uses the other available hours in a practical way.

Make sure that you schedule enough time for these activities so that you can include your children, getting value-buck fellowship with them. They will be a detriment to your time productivity when they are young, but remember that eventually they will take over those jobs from you, freeing up a considerable amount of your time for other projects.

Sunday Schedule

A daily schedule adapts to Sunday as well. It all depends on your family and the structure of your life. That is why you shouldn't use the sample schedule but make up one that fits your own family's needs. Knowing Sundays are going to be different for most families, I will still show a sample one for Sunday.

Sample Sunday Schedule

Wake up	5:30 a.m.
Personal time in the Word and prayer	5:40-6:50
Get ready for the day	6:50-7:15
Breakfast	7:15-7:30
Optional time to study Sunday School lesson	7:30-8:20
Prepare for church	8:20-8:30
Church	8:30-12:30 p.m.
Start meetings with children	12:30-1:00
Lunch	1:00-1:30
Meetings with children	1:30-2:30
Naps	2:30-4:30
Family walk or talk	4:30-5:30
Help with light dinner prep/Eat/Cleanup	5:30-6:30

Schedule continued on next page

Sample Sunday Schedule Continued

Family Bible time	6:30-7:15
Time with family	7:15-8:15
Pray with children	8:15-8:30
Scripture memory	8:30-8:45
Personal reading	8:45-9:15
Get ready for bed/Talk to/Pray with Wife	9:15-10:00
Bedtime	10:00 p.m.

More Examples

Let's look at an evening schedule for a dad with young children and a possible schedule scenario. If you work swing shift rather than the usual 8 to 5, the evening schedule would simply be shifted to an early afternoon schedule. If you work some other hours, you would schedule your home hours in a similar fashion, whenever they occur. This schedule will apply to the hours you have at home to invest in your family and household projects.

If we assume that Dad is home from work at 5:45 p.m. and in bed at 10:30 p.m., the time budget allows him four hours and forty-five minutes to work with. Some parts of that schedule are cut and dried, such as the time to eat. Other aspects are more fluid. Remember that we start with the known priorities and their amounts of time:

Greet family/Change clothes	15 minutes
Eat dinner	30 minutes
Family Bible time	45 minutes
Prepare for bed	30 minutes

Now look at the other priorities for evening time. If you have younger children, you will probably help your wife with the kitchen cleanup after eating and include your children with you. Working together will let you train the children to work and give you fellowship with your family. This would likely take thirty minutes.

With little children in the family, weather permitting, outdoor family exercise would be another beneficial priority for your time, so you could put on your list a family walk. A walk will help the children wear off energy to help them get tired enough to settle down for their night's sleep. It is also another opportunity to accrue value bucks by letting you have talking time with your wife while getting needed exercise for both of you. If the walk is a thirty-minute walk, you will need to schedule forty-five minutes because of the time it will take to get everyone ready. This exercise time could be traded out for a grocery shopping trip for Dad and the children once a week if it were combined with another block of time.

Helping to put the children to bed can easily require a thirty-minute block of time, but it could include praying together and reading aloud. Adding up the time that is left in the evening leaves one hour. That could be available time for computer work, a small house-repair project, family finances, ministry preparation, or whatever is on the list that you are keeping to direct your time when you have a block of time available.

Your schedule might look like this:

Greet family/Change clothes	5:45 p.m.
Dinner	6:00
Cleanup	6:30
Walk (Tues/grocery shopping/Thurs/every 5 weeks haircuts)	7:00
Family Bible time (8:15 on Tuesday)	7:45
Help w/children's bedtime prep/Pray/Read aloud (No read aloud on Tuesday)	8:30
Project time (M&W/E-mail, T&F/Car or house project, TH/Finances, Sat/Date time)	9:00
Prepare for bed/Pray with Wife	10:00
Bedtime	10:30 p.m.

Obviously, there are many activities that could be included in an evening schedule. That is why prayer is so important in discerning what your priorities are and then setting the schedule up accordingly.

A Sample Evening Schedule with Older Children

Since our children are not very young any more, I will use my evening schedule as an example for this category.

Dinner	5:30 p.m.
Computer (if time permits)	6:00
Family Bible time	6:30
Family music practice or Errands if needed	7:30
E-mail/Computer work	8:30
Pray with boys and talk	8:45
E-mail/Desk	9:15
Prepare for bed (Lock up house/Brush teeth/Read Scripture and pray with Teri)	9:30
Bedtime	10:00 p.m.

There are evenings when I need to make a run to a home supply store or cut hair. On those nights we skip family music practice, and I might have to preempt my final computer work. There are occasional nights when I have a house project that needs attention for which I might skip family music time. However, the goal of a schedule is to consistently follow it. If we never have family music time and I am always doing something else, then my schedule needs to change.

When the children are older, there is more flexibility in evening activities because the children need less oversight and are more capable of doing things for themselves. My children are at an age where they are completely responsible for dinner cleanup. This frees Teri and me for other activities. Since several children help with the cleanup, it goes quickly, and they can fellowship while they work. We no longer need to be involved in helping the children get ready for bed. Again, this frees up time that I didn't have when the children were younger.

A Real-Life Example

Here is a comment from our survey that details a dad's specific time problems. Let's look at how he could use a schedule to help him.

"My husband has the type of job that requires him to be at meetings a large percentage of the time, but he is still expected to complete regular work, too. As a result, after eating dinner and spending a little time with the children, he is on his work computer for the rest of the evening. I have struggled with this in the past because our couple time is limited, but I have accepted it as a necessary phase that we must work through. I really would like to become more involved in our new church, but would like for us to be together when we are involved. I would love for us to have family devotions, but I don't want to add something else to his plate and make him feel frustrated that he can't keep up with everything."

Although we don't know the ages of his children, here is what he might try for an evening schedule.

Greet family/Change clothes	6:00 p.m.
Eat dinner	6:15
Work	6:45
Family Bible time/Pray with children	8:00
Work	8:40
Time with Wife	9:45
Bedtime	10:30 p.m.

This schedule doesn't allow him time for his personal projects, but it gives him Bible and prayer time with his family and time to talk with his wife. He will then need to be very diligent with his Saturdays to stay caught up with other responsibilities. It also lets him have a significant amount of time for the work that he brings home. I would challenge him to try to limit his work to one hour faithfully scheduled and utilized each evening. Perhaps that amount of extra work would give him the ability to keep up and still allow some time in the evening for other family time or projects.

What if Dad looked at our suggested schedule and said, "That won't work for me because the work time is segmented, and I need to have an uninterrupted block of time." My first thought would be that in normal work environments our time is interrupted constantly by phone calls and people walking up to talk or make requests. A mental adjustment is necessary to have a good attitude about using every minute efficiently even if the schedule can't produce the ideal circumstance.

There is no doubt that uninterrupted larger blocks of time can be more productive than several smaller blocks. It could be that evaluation and experimentation would lead to other ways to organize the evening so that Dad's work could be scheduled in a solid block of time. However, if Dad's heart is focused on the fact that discipling the children is his highest calling, he will have a good attitude toward making the right decisions on how his time is utilized.

Don't Put It Off

It is my desire that by giving you concrete examples of how schedules are set up for particular needs, you will be motivated to put together a schedule for your time. Use these examples to spur your thinking about how a schedule will work best with the parameters and needs of your life. Don't put it off. Begin right now by praying and making your list of activities that you believe the Lord would have you do—both a daily and a weekly list. Use that information to make a rough daily Saturday and Sunday schedule. Then fill in the open blocks of time in the rough schedule and begin to use your schedule. You might find that within just a short amount of time, you have all of your schedules completed and ready to implement. I believe that if you will be determined to be consistent with following a schedule, you will experience untold blessings in your life concerning your time management, with a ripple effect into all other areas of your life and your family's life as well.

Stop the excuses! What excuse will you have when your children are gone? Schedule your life now.

I hated schedules. I thought they were a joke especially on a farm, but through the Lord and your book I realized that this was a surrender issue for me. I need to surrender my time to the Lord.

A Challenging Conclusion

Teri and I have eaten by candlelight a few times. I find a burning candle in a dark room quite fascinating. The thin flame extending upward from the wick seems to have a life of its own as it moves about by slight changes in air currents around it. The light from something so small is still bright enough to cast shadows on the walls. Its purpose is to give off light, and it will consume itself in the process. Once lit, it is only a matter of time before its "life" is over and another must take its place. Our lives are all too similar to a candle. The flame is lit, and it is only a matter of time before we have burned ourselves out. Will we be ever so careful with the precious amount of time that the Lord has given us to be lights on this earth? Will we redeem our time? Will we learn to number our days?

Looking for Peace

Dads today feel such pressure over how they will use their time. In the midst of the storm, the Lord Jesus promises us peace and an abundant life. Since Jesus' promises are always true, then why is it more Christian men don't have peace? "No man that warreth entangleth himself with the affairs of *this* life; that he may please him who hath chosen him to be a soldier" (2 Timothy 2:4). Sadly, many Christian men have entangled themselves in the affairs of this life. Some examples of the affairs of this life would be wasting time, pursuing entertainment or recreation, and focusing too much on work while neglecting their vital priority of raising their children in the nurture and admonition of the Lord. They are not living to please the Lord, Who has called them to the battle. Therefore, their lives are filled with pressure and the absence of peace.

Many claim that they are free in Christ to enjoy the non-sinful pleasures of this world. In Galatians, however, we read that our freedom is from sin, not to do what we want: "For, brethren, ye have been called unto liberty; only *use* not liberty for an occasion to the flesh, but by love serve one another" (Galatians 5:13). We are purchased by our Lord's blood, to be His bride and to be busy about His business in serving others. If we want His peace, we must follow His rules.

"Come unto me, all *ye* that labour and are heavy laden, and I will give you rest. Take my yoke upon you, and learn of me; for I am meek and lowly in heart: and ye shall find rest unto your souls. For my yoke *is* easy, and my burden is light" (Matthew 11:28-30). His yoke is easy, and His burden is light. We look at that yoke and burden from our perspective, but it looks hard and heavy because we have become used to living by making our own choices for how we spend our time. We won't let go, and therefore, we never experience the rest that Jesus says He will give us.

Testing and Warfare

Could it be that the time pressures and time robbers in our lives are being used by God to test us, to prove us, and to train us in spiritual battle? Look with me for a moment at Israel.

"Now these *are* the nations which the LORD left, to prove Israel by them, *even* as many *of Israel* as had not known all the wars of Canaan; Only that the generations of the children of Israel might know, to teach them war, at the least such as before knew nothing thereof; . . . And they were to prove Israel by them, to know whether they would hearken unto the commandments of the LORD, which he commanded their fathers by the hand of Moses" (Judges 3:1-4).

The Lord could have wiped out all the nations residing in the Promised Land before bringing His chosen people into it. There would have been no battles, no pain, no sorrow, no death, and no hardship for the Israelites. However, God had two purposes for leaving those adversaries in the land. He wanted to test His people's hearts to see if they would be steadfast in obeying Him. He also was using the warfare to teach the Israelites to fight.

I think God is doing something similar in our lives. He hasn't taken away the temptation we have to focus on ourselves, to want to be entertained, to waste our time, and to make our own choices. He desires to use those enemies in our lives to test our hearts and to teach us to do spiritual battle.

"For to this end also did I write, that I might know the proof of you, whether ye be obedient in all things" (2 Corinthians 2:9). Will we be obedient? We are given that choice. "Know ye not, that to whom ye yield yourselves servants to obey, his servants ye are to whom ye obey; whether of sin unto death, or of obedience unto righteousness?" (Romans 6:16). We can yield to self or to obedience. Most are not willing to make the sacrifices that will be involved to yield to righteousness. It seems too hard right now, and they put it off for another day, willing to live for the present with guilt, stress, and discouragement.

The spiritual war is raging, and the stakes are high. Each decision we make concerning our time usage is a training battle the Lord has placed in our lives. We see in the Word what constitutes these battles and how we fight them.

"For though we walk in the flesh, we do not war after the flesh: (For the weapons of our warfare *are* not carnal, but mighty through God to the pulling down of strong holds;) Casting down imaginations, and every high thing that exalteth itself against the knowledge of God, and bringing into captivity every thought to the obedience of Christ" (2 Corinthians 10:3-5). The battlefront is behind our eyes—in our minds with our thoughts. Will we bring our thoughts into the obedience of Christ, or will we continue to think as we always have?

The Biblical Role Model

In our survey asking questions about men's time struggles, the following comment reflects one that was made many times. *"My husband is a first-generation Christian and doesn't have older, godly role models to follow in regard to being a husband, father, etc."* Many men hunger for someone, who has victoriously walked the path before, to lead and direct them in their spiritual journey as a Christian husband and father. They know they only have one go at it, and they want to get it right.

Most of us have grown up in non-Christian homes or ones where religion was confined to attending church on Sunday morning. We watched our fathers go to work, come home to watch TV all evening, and get up the next morning to start over, or something similar. There was no passion in their lives for the things of God. Because they lived for their free time in front of the television, we joined them, and we grew up feeling that was what we needed to do after a hard day's work as well. If our dads loved flying, we loved it. If they lived for their hunting trips, we did too. It all revolved around what Dad felt he needed to make him happy.

Through the Word, we begin to discover that life in Christ is different. Jesus, the Living Word, is our role model. "As ye have therefore received Christ Jesus the Lord, *so* walk ye in him: Rooted and built up in him, and stablished in the faith, as ye have been taught, abounding therein with thanksgiving" (Colossians 2:6-7). Many Christians are not rooted in the Word, and they simply do what everyone else does. If we look to them for answers, we will follow the same vanities and experience the same emptiness.

Let me share with you the first of three testimonies to encourage you on the changes you can expect in your family if you will but begin to number your days and redeem the time.

"I used to spend a lot of time on 'time robbers' instead of on the Word of God and investing in the eternal destiny of my family. My wake-up call came during the Maxwells' marriage conference. The results:

• Over 20 trash bags of DVDs, video games and equipment, one 55" HDTV, and around 1,000 books. My wife and I estimate we threw away over $10,000 worth of 'rubbish' that we had accumulated.

• Daily Bible and prayer for my wife and me

• Daily Bible time for the whole family

• Less 'worldly' noise in my life, and more clarity about God's will for my family and my life.

• Daily Bible time has made a HUGE difference in our lives. It has been one year since we started Bible time, and we haven't missed a day yet. I was on the road for five days, but we did them over webcam and on the phone when I was at the airport. We've done them as early as noon and as late as 10 p.m.—late for little ones

that need to be in bed at 8. They're getting it. The four-year-old knows his ten commandments, and all the books of the Bible in order, and understands some key concepts. I love to see them grow in knowledge."

Is It Unrealistic?

I know that some who read this book will mock. They will declare that time management such as I describe here is unrealistic and unreasonable. My heart goes out not only to them but also to their wives and children. There is such a heart cry from families yearning for Dad to spend time with them, love them, teach them the Word—to be the spiritual leader in the home.

"Wherefore gird up the loins of your mind, be sober, and hope to the end for the grace that is to be brought unto you at the revelation of Jesus Christ; As obedient children, not fashioning yourselves according to the former lusts in your ignorance: But as he which hath called you is holy, so be ye holy in all manner of conversation; Because it is written, Be ye holy; for I am holy" (1 Peter 1:13-16). I believe what I have shared with you concerning redeeming time, numbering our days, and time management is simply part of being an obedient child, walking in holiness—with nothing unrealistic or unreasonable about it—except that it is the calling of God on our lives.

"Wherefore he saith, Awake thou that sleepest, and arise from the dead, and Christ shall give thee light. See then that ye walk circumspectly, not as fools, but as wise, Redeeming the time, because the days are evil" (Ephesians 5:14-16). Many dads are spiritually asleep. Christ tells us to wake up, and He will give us light—direction. We are given a choice. We can redeem the time, or we can focus on ourselves, chasing vanities and time robbers.

Here is an example of a dad who has decided to make the changes in his life that we are encouraging you to consider. Look at the results in their family.

*"**Down with the beast**—Since we have removed the beast from our home and all video games, I think our family is nicer to each other, and I do not miss being asked: 'Can we play video games, now?' 'Can we watch TV now?' The children have not asked even once if we could have the TV or video games back! But the change has not been without trouble. I found out after removing the beast that I had been deceived by the beast. I thought that my children enjoyed being 'together' and playing 'together.' The very sad truth was that they were willing to be with their siblings and 'play with' them just because they were watching TV or playing a video game 'together.' After learning this sad truth, we made a rule for a couple of days that you must be with another sibling at ALL times (eating, playing, chores, Bible time). We have two boys and two girls, and we keep pairing them up with different children. We have started to allow them some time alone again, but it was a hard fight for a couple of days.*

*"**Family Bible Time**—Family Bible time has been completely wonderful. The children look forward to family Bible time, and we are learning a ton from God's Word. I find that the children have started to use Scripture and things that we talked about in family Bible time throughout the day."*

Whom to Serve?

". . . as for me and my house, we will serve the LORD" (Joshua 24:15). I join Joshua in making this declaration. I am determined to manage every minute the Lord Jesus has given me for His honor and His glory. It takes courage. It takes self-sacrifice. It takes self-discipline. It takes standing against what is popular. It takes reliance on the Holy Spirit. However, the fruit is worth it all.

I have lived the other way, and I have no desire to return. I enjoyed the leeks of Egypt, and the pleasures of sin for a season, but I found a better way. "By faith Moses, when he was come to years, refused to be called the son of Pharaoh's daughter; Choosing rather to suffer affliction with the people of God, than to enjoy the pleasures of sin for a season; Esteeming the reproach of Christ greater riches than the treasures in Egypt: for he had respect unto the recompence of the reward" (Hebrews 11:24-26).

When you picked this book up to read it, you probably thought I was going to give you five steps to effectively managing your time. Instead I may have shocked you with talk of vital priorities, time robbers, and schedules. Be determined that you will learn, from the Lord Jesus, to number your days and redeem your time. Look to His Word for the truth of what I have shared with you in this book. Even if it goes against your flesh, which I think it will, choose obedience and the blessings that come with it. Haven't you lived long enough already under the curses of time pressure, feeling stressed, and realizing your failures?

Any man can make these choices that I am convinced lead to the abundant life Jesus promised us. We will bless our families as we make these changes in our lives. They will gain back a husband and father who has time for them and is their spiritual leader. We will disciple our children and be the godly role models to them that we have longed for, but missed, in our own lives. "I have no greater joy than to hear that my children walk in truth" (3 John 1:4). While that may be a man's greatest joy, it is likely his greatest sorrow to lose his children to the snares of the world. There is no heartache like it. In the busyness of life, it is possible to continually put off investing time in our children, waiting for a more convenient time when things settle down. Will that time ever come? If it does, will it be too late?

Are we giving our children an appetite for the things of the world, vanities, and wasted time by the time robbers we have allowed to steal away our time? God holds us accountable. "And, ye fathers, provoke not your children to wrath: but bring them up in the nurture and admonition of the Lord" (Ephesians 6:4). I have used this verse continually throughout the book. Take it to heart.

I want to share one final testimony of what can happen in a family when Dad decides to number his days.

"The beasts are gone!! I can hardly contain myself! To hear that the Lord had worked on my husband's heart through you to rid us of these awful things was just amazing!! After he put them out, my four-year-old daughter said to him, 'But Daddy, what about the shows YOU like to watch?' And he said, 'Some things are more important to me than my TV shows. Do you know what they are?' And she quietly pointed to her own chest, and he nodded his head. They both cried and hugged. I type this with happy tears, too. God is so good. I feel like a weight has been lifted off our entire home! My husband and the girls made a list of the things they want to create and do together. We have a new lease on life and this is just the beginning!

"We have been set free. Our lives are forever changed. My husband's heart has turned toward his wife and his children. My children wake up asking for Daddy. Our testimony to God's blessing was amazing before, but now it's tremendous. We hear Him, we SEE Him move in our lives. We feel clean.

"By the way, my husband and I feel like we've gotten the life back we never knew we lost. Our girls' personalities blossomed, almost instantly! They are so funny and keep telling us how much they love us. I almost always had to say it first, and now they say it all day long.

"They have made a REAL birdhouse with Daddy, out of wood and nails, etc., to be painted pink (of course) this weekend. Creativity has led to more creativity in all of us. We played hide-n-seek outside last night so long we all almost fell over laughing from exhaustion. AND, I now can get all the homeschool stuff out of my closet and put into the beast's old home, the huge armoire. I've never had so much storage real estate in my life! Almost every single thing I've been praying for (and crying about) for months was answered by God with even more blessing than I could have ever even imagined. The days keep getting better. I am literally dancing through the house!"

Implementing a Scheduled Life

Many men are not interested in developing a schedule and using it. I was in that category myself for a long time. However, with the demands we find ourselves faced with, it almost becomes imperative that we have a schedule to manage our time. The experience of those who move from no scheduling, me included, to scheduling testifies to this. Often when a dad hasn't been using a schedule, he thinks it won't be workable or feasible. Remember, we said earlier that the greatest hindrance to a dad using a schedule is right behind his eyes—his thinking that he won't be able to do it. Those thoughts emanate from his lack of experience in scheduling. When you put together a schedule and start to use it, you will find it amazing how different, in a very positive way, the reality actually is from how you imagined it would be.

I want to challenge you to give scheduling a try. In the book for moms on scheduling, we give them a kit to help them with their schedules because they were scheduling for themselves and for the children—a much more complicated schedule than a dad will be making. That Scheduling Kit is a motivation for the moms to work on a schedule. You don't have a Scheduling Kit, but all you have to do is get out your computer or paper and pencil to begin getting your schedule made up. The examples are in the appendix to give you a pattern and ideas, but your schedule will be prayerfully designed under the direction of the Lord Jesus Christ, especially for you, your responsibilities, and your time demands.

Put your schedule together and use it for two weeks. See for yourself the changes and benefits you will gain. I believe you will move from chaos and stress to order, peace, and productivity. The blessings you realize from the schedule will be the motivation to keep you using it.

Redeeming the Time

The continual prayer of my heart is that men would become serious in their relationships with Jesus Christ. As that happens, lives are changed and families are transformed. Learn to number your days in an obedient walk with Jesus Christ. Choose to redeem your time. He will give you a vision for your life and your family's lives. He will direct you in your time management. He will supply you with grace and strength to release your time robbers. He will furnish you with a workable schedule. Through it all, He will grant you peace and the abundant life. Our time is our most valuable possession. What will we do with it?

> I think the main question that a man needs to answer after reading this book is WHERE is his heart? How is he using the precious treasure that is his time? Matthew 6:19-21

Appendix

12 Sample Schedules
from 12 dads

Dad 1 Schedule

Time	Mon-Fri	Saturday	Sunday
5:15 a.m.	Shower/Prepare for day	Sleep	Sleep
5:30	Shower/Prepare for day	Prepare for day	Sleep
5:45	Breakfast	Breakfast	Sleep
6:00	Bible/Prayer		Sleep
6:30	Commute/(Bible on MP3)		Sleep
7:00	Commute/(Bible on MP3)		Sleep
7:30	Work	Work in table grape vineyard	Shower/Prepare for day
7:45	Work		Breakfast
8:15	Work		Bible/Prayer
8:45	Work		Sermon prep
9:15	Work		Leave for church
9:30	Work		
10:00	Work		Church
10:30	Work		or
11:00	Work		Family Bible
11:30	Work		
12:00 p.m.	Lunch	Lunch	Lunch prep
12:30	Work	Lunch	Lunch
12:45	Work	Bible/Prayer	Lunch
1:15	Work	Sermon prep	
2:15	Work	Sermon prep	Fellowship or Family time
4:00	Shut down computer/Walk to car	Projects	Fellowship or Family time
4:15	Commute/(Bible on MP3)	Projects	
5:15	Errands on the way home/or Ride fence	Projects	
5:30	Greet family/Change clothes	Projects	Review week w/Linda
6:00	Dinner	Dinner	Dinner
6:45	Review evening plans	Family time	Help clean up
7:00	E-mail	Family time	

Evening breakdown (Mon–Fri), Saturday, Sunday:

Time	M	Tues	W	TH	Fri	Saturday	Sunday
7:15	M/Finances	Tues Ride fence	W/Music	TH/Ride fence	Fri/Date night	Family time	Music
7:45	M/Ride fence	Tues Ride fence	W/Music	TH/Ride fence	Fri/Date night	Family time	Music
8:00	M/Ride fence	Tues Ride fence	W/Music	TH/Ride fence	Fri/Date night	Family time	Review with Jonathan
8:15	M/Ride fence	Tues Ride fence	W/Ride fence	TH/Ride fence	Fri/Date night	Family time	Review with Cathy Jo
8:30			W/Ride fence	TH/Call Mom		Family time	Read as a family
8:45			W/Ride fence	TH/Call Mom		Family time	Read as a family

Time	All
9:00	Family Bible
9:45	Ready for bed
10:00 p.m.	Sleep

Two children; boy (19), girl (17)

Corporate job and a small farm

Appendix

Dad 2 Schedule

	Mon-Fri	Saturday	Sunday
5:00 a.m.	Get dressed/Breakfast	Sleep	Sleep
5:15	Bible/Prayer		
5:30		Get dressed	
5:45		Breakfast/Bible/Prayer	
6:00		Gather supplies for	Shower
7:00	Work	project	Bible/Prayer/Eat
7:30			Awaken family
8:00		Go to store for supplies	Barn chores
8:30			
8:45		Coffee with Wife	Gather church supplies
9:00		Delegate jobs to	
9:15	Work	family/Assist with major or	Start loading for church
		minor projects	Leave for church
9:30			
12:00 p.m.		Lunch	Church
1:30		Resume morning project	Home/Put church things away
1:45		or begin a second one	Lunch
2:00			Nap
3:00			Outside with
4:00	Work	Clean up/Give Wife a list of what is needed for next week	children
4:30		Time with children	Walk around farm with Wife/Talk/Discuss plans/events
5:30		Help finish supper prep	
6:00		Supper	Supper
6:30		Supervise bath time/Help	
7:00	Supper	children prep for	Family activities
7:15	Time with children	Sunday/Tidy house	
7:45	Shower	Family Bible	
8:00	Family Bible		Family Bible
8:15		Help put	
8:30		children to bed	Help put
8:45	Help put children to bed	Check barn for night/Fill	children in bed
9:00	Work prep	waterers and feeders	Work prep
9:15	Phone calls	Time with Wife	Phone calls
9:30	Time with Wife		Time with Wife
10:00 p.m.		Sleep	

Six children; girl (10), boy (8), girl (8), girl (6), girl (4), boy (1 ½)
Self-employed with family business

Dad 3 Schedule

	Mon-Fri	Saturday	Sunday
5:00 a.m.	Run/Shower/Dress	Sleep	Sleep
5:50	Breakfast		
6:00	Bible/Prayer	Shower/Dress/Bible/Prayer	
6:30	Commute/Memorization	Bible/Prayer	
7:00		Breakfast/Clean up	
8:30	Work	Projects/Errands	Help children prepare for church
9:30		Shopping	
			Church
12:00 p.m.	Work	Lunch/Clean up	Lunch/Clean up
1:00		Nap/Quiet time/Reading	
3:00			
4:00	Commute/Prayer	Projects	Family activities
4:30	Greet/Change clothes		
4:45	Play with children		
5:00	Dinner/Clean up/Make lunch		
5:30			
6:00	Family Bible	Dinner/Clean up	Dinner/Clean up
6:30	Family time/Gardening/Small projects	Family Bible	
7:00	with the children/Grocery shopping/Play w/children and give baths every 3rd night	Family time/Baths	Family time
7:30	Children to bed/Prayer		
8:00	Daily rotation (Finances/Laundry/House cleaning/Reading/E-mail)	Date night with Karin	Catch up time
8:30			
9:00	Pray with Karin/Ready for bed		
9:30	Sleep/Dreams of the Lord		Pray with Karin/Ready for bed
10:00 p.m.		Pray with Karin/Ready for bed	Sleep/Dreams of the Lord

Three children; boy (6), boy (4), girl (2)

Corporate job IT

Dad 4 Schedule

	Mon-Thur	Friday	Saturday	Sunday
5:40 a.m.	Wake up			
5:50	Bible/Prayer			Bible/Prayer
6:15	Prepare for work		Prepare for day	
6:30	Walk dog w/children		Walk dog w/family	
6:40	Commute			
7:00			Breakfast	Breakfast
7:30				Clean up
8:00			Grocery shopping	Family Bible
8:30	Work		Put away groceries	
9:15				Prep for church
10:00			Project #1	Nursing Home
10:10				Church
11:30			Lunch	
12:00 p.m.			Lunch cleanup	Emily meeting
12:30				Lunch
1:00				Clean up
1:30	Work		Project #2	Hanna meeting
2:00				Joel meeting
2:30				Naps
3:00			Project #3	Family time
4:00				(walk, etc)
5:00	Commute home		Help w/dinner prep	Dinner
5:15	Help w/dinner prep	Change clothes		
5:30	Dinner	Mow lawn	Dinner	
6:00	Clean up		Clean up	Clean up
6:30	Help children brush teeth	Clean pool	Help children brush teeth	Family Bible
6:45	Bible time		Family Bible	
7:00		Dinner		Family Bible
7:30	Family Bible	Clean up	Music	Sing or Guitars
7:45		Help children brush teeth		
8:00	Pray/Tuck children in	Family Bible	Pray/Tuck children in	
8:30	E-mail	Pray/Tuck children in	E-mail	Memory verses
9:00	Job hunt w/Kate			Personal reading
9:30	Read/Pray/Talk w/Kate			
10:00 p.m.	Bedtime			

Four children; boy (11), girl (9), girl (4), girl (9 mo.)

Employed as a project manager

Dad 5 Schedule

	Mon-Fri	Saturday	Sunday
4:30 a.m.	Bible/Prayer		
5:10	Go to farm/Milk and feed animals		
7:15	Shower		
7:30	Family Bible/Breakfast w/family		
8:15	Commute to work	Work on farm	Misc
8:30	Work		Time with Cheryl and devotions
11:30		Home projects Children projects Farm projects	Visiting friends or family
4:00 p.m.	Return home	Dinner with family	
4:15	Greet all/Dinner/Spend time with Cheryl		
5:00	Work on farm with children		
7:30	Tuck younger children in bed	Church and worship	Tuck younger children in bed
7:45	Time with older children/Games/Talking		Time with older children
8:45	Bills and Record keeping—Tues/Thurs With older children/Projects—M/W/Fri		Projects
9:30	Prepare for bed/Quiet reading time		Prepare for bed Reading time
10:00 p.m.	Sleep	Tuck children in/Sleep	Sleep

Nine children; boy (18), girl (16), girl (15), boy (13), girl (9), girl (7), girl (7), girl (4), girl (1)

Works a dairy farm and has a city job

Dad 6 Schedule

	Tues/Wed/Thurs	Mon/Fri/Sat	Sunday
7:00 a.m.	Prayer/Bible		
7:15	Bible		
7:30	Shower/Breakfast/Online Scripture study		
7:45	Scripture study/Get ready to go		Continue Bible study
8:00	Project block 1 with children		Get ready to go
9:00			
10:00	Project block 2 Tues/Wed/Th Limo prep Mon/Fri/Sat		Church
12:00 p.m.	Family dinner/Bible quiz w/children		Weekly picnic at Creation Museum/Family Bible
12:15	Family Bible time A		Creation Museum
1:00	Project block 3	Same as Mon/Wed/Thurs or limousine job. Review Scriptures when waiting for customers.	
3:00	Project block 4		Farmer's Market
5:00	Project block 5		Head to Grandma's/Dinner
6:00			Dinner & Bible quiz w/Grandma
6:30			Call family in FL at Grandma's
7:00	Family bike ride to Grandma's or		Head home
7:15	supper at home		
7:30	Picnic at Grandma's, Bible quiz, OR work if a job comes up		Plan for week
7:45	Games at Grandma's OR work		
8:00			Prepare for bed
8:30	Family Bible time B at Grandma's		
9:00	Bike ride home		
9:30	Help with children's before-bed routine		Relax or Sleep
9:45	Pray with children/Kiss goodnight		
10:00 p.m.	Change/Time with Dara/Bed		

Seven children; girl (13), boy (11), boy (9), boy (7), boy (6), girl (4), boy (1)
Self-employed with two businesses

Dad 7 Schedule

	Mon-Fri	Saturday	Sunday
6:30 a.m.	Get dressed	Sleep	Sleep
6:45	Bible/Prayer		
7:15	Breakfast	Get dressed	Get dressed
7:30	Drive to work (memorize Scripture)	Bible/Prayer	Bible/Prayer
8:00	Work	Breakfast/Clean up	Breakfast/Clean up
8:45		Computer time	Help get children ready for church
9:00		Projects or ministry time	Church
12:00 p.m.	Lunch (optionally run errands, check e-mail, write out Scripture to memorize)	Lunch and clean up	
1:00	Work		
1:30		Projects or ministry time	Individual conferences w/boys
2:30			Lunch
3:30		Family walk/Fellowship	Fellowship with other believers or project work
4:00		Individual conferences with the girls	
4:30			
5:00	Drive home (memorize Scripture)		
5:30	Greet family/Check e-mail/Do finances	Dinner and clean up	
5:45	Dinner and clean up		
6:30	Family Bible	Family Bible	Dinner and clean up
7:15	House or car projects	Projects or ministry time	
7:30			
8:00	Time with children (play time or family walk time)		Family Bible
8:20	Math with boys		
8:45	Good night and prayer w/children	Review Bible verses w/children for Sunday	Good night and prayer w/children
9:00		Good night and prayer w/children	
9:15	Talk/Walk/Plan/Pray with Wife		
10:15	Get ready for bed		
10:30 p.m.	Sleep		

Four children; boy (10), boy (9), girl (7), girl (3)

Employed programmer

Dad 8 Schedule

	Mon	Tues-Fri	Saturday	Sunday
6:30 a.m.	Wake up		Wake up	Wake up
6:45	Bible time		Bible time	Bible time
7:15			Children's breakfast/Clean up	
7:30	Work		Children showered/Dressed	
8:00				
			Projects	Sunday school prep/Commentary (biweekly)
9:00				
9:45	Work		Lunch prep/Eat	Church
11:30			Clean up	
12:30 p.m.			Boys down for naps	Lunch
1:00				
2:00			Projects	Naps
4:00				Family meeting (individual)
4:30	Family Bible	Help Wife[1]	Projects/Nap[2]	Make grocery list/Walk to store
			Dinner	
5:15	Church meetings		Dinner	Grocery shop
5:30		Dinner		
6:00				
6:30		Projects	Family activity: Read Walk/Other	Dinner
7:00			Family Bible	
7:45			Bed prep for boys: brush teeth, etc	
8:00			Proverb/Prayer with boys	
8:30		Projects	Sunday School prep	Upcoming week discussion w/wife
9:00	Reading			Computer and reading
9:30	Computer maintenance			
10:00	Computer time		Computer/Reading	
10:30	Wife time/Personal hygiene			
11:00				
11:30 p.m.	Sleep			

1. Help Wife catch up on things: school with boys/grade, clean, watch children while she makes dinner, take children on errands, prepare dinner myself, etc.

2. Depending on sleep from previous week–baby, etc.

Five children; boy (6), boy (5), boy (3), boy (2), boy (4 mo.)

Computer consultant

Dad 9 Schedule

	Monday-Saturday	Sunday
5:00 a.m.	Pray/Bible	Pray/Bible
5:30		
5:45		Milking/Farm chores
6:00		
6:30		
7:00		
7:30		
7:50		Change clothes/Drive home
8:00	Milking/Farm chores	Get ready for church
8:30		Drive to church
9:00		
9:30		
10:00		Church/Fellowship
10:30		
11:00		
11:30		
11:45	Change clothes/Go home	
12:00 p.m.	Eat/Clean up	Drive home
12:30		Lunch/Clean up
1:00	Family Bible	
1:30	Change and leave to farm	Family Bible
1:45	Summer farm work i.e. field/yard	
2:00	work/winter prep	Bible study with friends
4:00		Play with the children
4:30		
5:30		
6:00	Milking chores with older children	Milking chores with older children
7:00		
7:30		
8:00		
8:30	Change clothes/Go home	
8:45	Greet little ones at home and help	Help get children to bed
9:00	Pray with children	
9:15	Eat/Shower	Eat/Shower
9:30	Bible time/Pray with Sandi	
10:15 p.m.		

Seven children; girl (12), boy (10), boy (7), boy (6), boy (4), girl (3), boy (1½)
   Dairy farmer

Dad 10 Schedule

	Mon-Fri	Saturday	Sunday
6:00 a.m.	Bible/Prayer	Bible/Prayer	Sleep
6:30	Workout	Workout	
7:00			Bible/Prayer
7:30	Breakfast	Bike ride	Shower
7:45	Shower		
8:00	Prep for work		Breakfast
8:15	Commute	Breakfast	
9:00	Work	Lawn work	Church
10:00		Car work i.e. wash vehicles	
10:30			
11:00		Misc project	
12:00 p.m.			Lunch
12:30		Lunch	
1:00			
1:30		Quiet work project	Nap
3:30			Time with Melanie
4:00			Play with Abigail
4:30	Commute		Family activity
5:00		Clean up	
5:15	Change clothes		
5:30	Play with Abigail	Dinner	Dinner
6:00	Dinner	Clean up/Abigail time	Social time with extended family
6:30	Clean up	Family activity	
7:00	Misc[1]		
7:30			
8:00	Family Bible		
8:30	Reading/Computer	Computer work/Internet research	With Melanie Read
9:00	Time w/Melanie		Sermon prep if needed
9:30 p.m.	Bed	Sermon prep if needed	

1. Misc–Tues/Grocery shopping, other days: finances/family walk/play with Abigail/work catch up/hospitality

One child; girl (1)

Self-employed IT consultant

Dad 11 Schedule

	Mon-Fri	Saturday	Sunday
6:00 a.m.	Get ready for work	Get ready for the day	
6:15	Bible/Prayer	Bible/Prayer	Bible/Prayer
6:45	Breakfast		
7:00	Prepare to leave	Children dressed/Assist with breakfast/Clean up	Children wake up/Get dressed
7:20	Leave for work (listen to podcasts: apologetics, debates, other)		Same as above
8:00	Work	Grocery shopping (family)	Breakfast/Clean up
8:30			Prepare for church
9:30		Put away food/Snack	Drive to church
10:00	Work		Drive to church
10:30		Project/Maintenance	
11:45	Work		Church
12:00 p.m.		Lunch prep/Eat	Drive home (eat lunch in car)
12:45		Flex time	
1:00	Work	Outside play with children	Change/Clean up
1:30			15 min. alone time with each child
2:00		Family rest time	
2:30		Time with Wife	
3:00		Bread making	Family rest time
3:40	Drive home		Teaching skills (baking, carpentry, correct use of a knife, etc.)
4:00		Take 1 child out for juice/donut and run errands OR house/car maintenance.	
4:20	Greet family/Change clothes		
4:30	Work/Play time w/children.[1]		
5:00			
5:30	Help with dinner prep		
6:00	Dinner		
6:20	Family Bible		
6:40	Cleaning: dishes/fold laundry/vacuum if needed		
7:15	Help children get ready for bed		
7:45	Read to younger/Tuck in/Hugs/Kisses		
8:00	Project time (2 nights teach music to boys)		
8:45	Bible time with older boys		
9:00	Paper work/Computer time		
10:00	Get ready for bed		
10:30 p.m.	Read/Talk in bed		

1. Involve children in whatever has to be done (i.e. restocking firewood, raking leaves, etc.) or play with them.

Six children; boy (10), boy (8), girl (5), boy (4), boy (2), girl (2 mo.)
Teacher

Dad 12 Schedule (Steve Maxwell)

	Mon-Fri	Saturday	Sunday
5:10 a.m.	Wake up/Talk/Get ready for day		
5:30	Memorize Scripture		Bible, prayer, and sermon prep
5:45	Read Bible/Pray in living room		
6:30	Walk with Teri		
7:45	Change/Breakfast		Family breakfast
8:00	Issues and direction (with individual children)		
8:15			Get ready
8:30	Music practice		Church
8:45	Work	Projects with the family	
11:15			Change
11:30			Meetings with children
12:00 p.m.	E-mail		
12:15	Lunch		Dinner
12:45	Work	Projects with the family	Meetings with children
2:30			Nap
4:30			Talk w/Teri
5:00			Talk w/family or Walk
5:30	Dinner		
6:00	Computer (if time permits)		Supper
6:30	Family Bible		
7:30	Family music practice or Errands with the family or Haircuts (every 5 weeks)		
8:30	E-mail		Family talk
8:45	Pray and talk with boys		
9:15	E-mail/Desk		Pray
9:30	Lock up house/Brush teeth/Talk, read NT chapter, pray with Teri		
9:45 p.m.			

Eight children (1 is married, 7 at home); boy (30), girl (27), boy (20), boy (18), girl (16), boy (14), girl (13)

Titus2.com ministry

Resources

Books and Audios (pages 238-253)
Free Monthly E-mail Articles by Steve & Teri
(Sign up by going to Titus2.com or calling (913) 772-0392.)
Websites (see below)

www.Titus2.com—Titus2.com provides information and resources to encourage, exhort, and equip Christian families. On the site you will find articles, information about the Maxwells' books, audios, and other resources. There are also sample children's chore charts and several master lists. Steve and Teri Maxwell write free monthly e-mail articles for Christian parents. The Dad's and Mom's Corners address issues that are at the heart of Christian families. You may sign up on the website.

www.ChorePacks.com—Ancillary to *Managers of Their Chores*. Book owners can download chore forms and make pre-reader chore cards. Also, check out ChoreWare, which greatly facilitates ChorePack development, on www.ChorePacks.com. ChoreWare is available for a small yearly subscription fee to owners of *Managers of Their Chores*.

www.FamiliesforJesus.com—A website dedicated to building up and challenging Christian families as they share Jesus with a lost and dying world.

www.HomeschooleCards.com—eCards designed to encourage homeschoolers and Christians in the Lord Jesus Christ!

www.PreparingSons.com—Work project center and more!

www.PreparingDaughters.com—A website especially for daughters who are striving to be women of God.

Preparing Sons
to Provide for a Single-Income Family
By Steven Maxwell

In today's world of two-income families, preparing a son to provide for a single-income family seems an overwhelming task. Christian parents will find it helpful to have a purpose and plan as they raise sons who will one day be responsible for supporting a family.

Steve Maxwell presents the groundwork for preparing your son to be a wage-earning adult. He gives practical suggestions and direction to parents for working with their sons from preschool age all the way to adulthood. You will be challenged to evaluate your own life and the example you are setting for your son.

As the father of eight children, five of them now wage-earning adults, Steve has gained valuable experience he openly shares with other parents. Learn these principles from a dad whose twenty-four-year-old homeschooled son purchased a home debt free a year before his marriage, and whose second son has done the same. Steve explains how it is possible for parents, with a willing commitment, to properly prepare their sons to provide for a single-income family.

"You are dealing with topics that no one I know of has dealt with as thoroughly and practically as you have." Dr. S. M. Davis

"Preparing Sons was a big blessing to my husband. All you ladies should get a copy for your husband and every church library needs one." Shelly

"I highly recommend the book for those of you who have not read it. I really appreciate all the obvious prayer, effort, and experience that went into making this book. The Lord is using it for His Glory in our family." Les

Preparing Sons is available in paperback or unabridged audiobook.

To order or for information visit: www.Titus2.com.
Or call: (913) 772-0392.

Keeping Our Children's Hearts
Our Vital Priority
by Steve & Teri Maxwell

Written for parents of young children to teenagers, this book shares the joys and outcomes of our vital priority—keeping our children's hearts. Rebellion and immorality are common among teens even within the Christian community. Does Scripture offer any path of hope for more than this for our children? What can parents do to direct their children toward godliness rather than worldliness? When does this process begin? What is the cost?

Steve and Teri Maxwell believe the key factors in raising children in the nurture and admonition of the Lord (Ephesians 6:4) are whether or not the parents have their children's hearts and what they are doing with those hearts. *Keeping Our Children's Hearts* offers direction and encouragement on this critically important topic.

Included in this book is a chapter co-authored by three of the adult Maxwell children concerning their thoughts, feelings, experiences, and outcomes of growing up in a home where their parents wanted to keep their hearts. There are also questions at the end of each chapter, which are thought provoking and helpful.

"The most complete and most balanced book I have read on how to raise children who won't rebel!" Dr. S. M. Davis

"This book is making me rethink what my purpose as a Christian, mother, and homeschooler should be." A mom

"The Scripture and its experiential application was encouraging and refreshing." A dad

"It truly is my top child rearing book now. You have brought together all the issues we have been striving to understand and achievements we hope to make with our children." A mom

To order or for information visit: www.Titus2.com.
Or call: (913) 772-0392.

Managers of Their Homes
A Practical Guide to Daily Scheduling for Christian Homeschool Families
By Steven and Teri Maxwell

A homeschool mother's greatest challenge may be "getting it all done." *Managers of Their Homes* offers solutions! Responses by families who have read *Managers of Their Homes* and utilized the Scheduling Kit indicate the almost unbelievable improvements they have realized.

Step-by-step instructions and a unique Scheduling Kit make setting up a daily schedule easily achievable for any homeschooling family. *"People have told me for years that I need a schedule, but every time I tried I couldn't get one to work. I always had problems fitting everything that needed to be done into one day. With your system, I am actually accomplishing more, and I have more time left over! The key to it is the great worksheets. They are invaluable."* Who wouldn't like to accomplish more and have time left over?

How does one schedule school time? Are you struggling with keeping up in areas such as laundry, dishes, or housekeeping? Does it seem like there is no time for you in the day? Do you feel stressed over the busyness of your days or not accomplishing all you want? It doesn't matter whether you have one child or twelve, this book will help you to plan your daily schedule.

Managers of Their Homes: A Practical Guide to Daily Scheduling for Christian Homeschool Families sets a firm biblical foundation for scheduling, in addition to discussing scheduling's numerous benefits. Chapter after chapter is filled with practical suggestions for efficient, workable ways to schedule a homeschooling family's days. Thirty real-life schedules in the Appendix give valuable insight into creating a personalized schedule. Also included is a special chapter by Steve for homeschool dads.

"My schedule has given me back my sanity!! I can't believe the way my life has changed since implementing a schedule." Tracy L.

"I had read almost every organizational book there was, and I still couldn't get to where I wanted to be until I applied this method!" Corrie

"In retrospect, having used the book, I would have paid $100 for it, if I could have known beforehand the tremendous benefits I would gain: peace in my busy home, and the ability my schedule gives me to accomplish the things I feel God wants me to do in my family." Tracy

"Your book helped to make our second year of homeschooling much smoother than the first! My three boys (8, 6, 6) have learned to be very helpful around the house and much more independent with their assignments for school. God has used your book to help prepare us for His plans! I feel totally confident and able to handle mothering and homeschooling and the new baby that will be arriving in January." Julie

"Making and using a schedule has helped me, and there were people who thought I was hopeless!" Sheri

"The advice and easy-to-apply information in the book are a must for large and small families alike. It is flexible, and anyone can do it; I love that. Even those who normally wouldn't be that structured are saying they love it, and it's so much fun. It's not just adding structure—it's advancing confidence!" Tina

"I'm probably the most unorganized person you've ever met. I'm always trying to do several things at one time. Anyway, your Scheduling Kit really did work. I know it was God's answer for me to have time for what I really wanted to do and what I really needed to do." Jacki

Moms who have applied these methods have gained new hope from MOTH (*Managers of Their Homes*). They have moved from chaos, stress, and disorganization to peace, contentment, and productivity. You can as well!

Softcover, 174 spiral-bound pages, oversized 8½ x 11 inch size, Scheduling Kit included.

To order or for information visit: www.Titus2.com.
Or call: (913) 772-0392.

Managers of Their Chores
A Practical Guide to Children's Chores
By Steven and Teri Maxwell

In the same way that *Managers of Their Homes* helped tens of thousands of moms "get it all done," *Managers of Their Chores* helps families conquer the chore battle. The book and included ChorePack system have the potential to revolutionize the way your family accomplishes chores. Whether you are chore challenged or a seasoned chore warrior, you will gain motivation and loads of practical advice on implementing a stress-free chore system.

Many questions arise as families look at the issue of chores: Should children be expected to do chores? How many chores should they have? What age do we begin assigning chores? How do we encourage our children to accomplish their work? Is there a biblical basis for chores? Do chores bring benefits or burdens to our children? There are a multitude of questions that arise when we begin to discuss chores. *Managers of Their Chores* tackles these questions, giving answers and direction.

Written by parents of eight, *Managers of Their Chores* begins with the biblical foundation for chores and the many benefits chores will bring to a child—both now and in the future. It moves into key factors in parents' lives that will affect a chore system. The book gives pertinent information about what kinds of chores should reasonably be done in a home with children.

One chapter is devoted to helping moms work with their preschoolers on chores. For those moms who say they have no idea where to even begin, the book develops various pieces of a chore system and how it can be set up. Aspects of accountability, rewards, and consequences are addressed. Finally, *Managers of Their Chores* provides step-by-step directions for setting up a ChorePack chore system.

Managers of Their Chores comes with all the ChorePack materials typically needed for four children, including ChorePacks, chore card paper, and a ChorePack holder. In the appendix of the book, you will find a chore library with more than 180 chores listed, forms for use and future photocopying, and sample chore assignments from eight families.

Help prepare your children—from preschoolers to teens—for life by teaching them to do chores.

"I can't believe how much time we have gained in our days now that we have our ChorePack system in place." A mom

"Its simplicity and ease of use encouraged independence and accountability at a young age." A mom

"My children are consistently doing their chores, and I am free from the daily burden of trying to do it all. Now I know it will get done at a certain time, and my children are growing in responsibility and independence and obedience. Thank you for such a wonderful resource." Heather

"It enabled the girls to do their own chores well, to not have to argue about whose turn it was or what they were going to do, and I didn't have to nag." A mom

"The fact is, we had our own chore system, but it wasn't working. The ChorePack system gave all of our children an excitement, and we saw immediate results. It helped with organization and them being able to do the chores on their own." A mom

ChoreWare, available to be purchased separately, is an Internet-based software developed to be used in conjunction with the *Managers of Their Chores* book, available only to *Managers of Their Chores* book owners. It allows you to create your chore system more efficiently than either handwriting it or using downloaded ChorePacks.com forms.

To order or for information visit: www.Titus2.com.
Or call: (913) 772-0392.

Managers of Their Schools
A Practical Guide to Homeschooling
By Steven and Teri Maxwell

Just as *Managers of Their Homes* and *Managers of Their Chores* have helped tens of thousands of moms "get it all done," *Managers of Their Schools* will facilitate families as they homeschool their children.

Have you ever wanted to sit down with an experienced homeschooling couple and ask them every question you could think of about homeschooling? *Managers of Their Schools: A Practical Guide to Homeschooling* is the next best thing. With eight children and twenty-three years as a homeschooling family, the Maxwells share their answers to the questions they are frequently asked.

This book is filled with practical information regarding how one family homeschools, what they use, why they do what they do, and how it all works for them. Steve and Teri set down the details of homeschooling in a real-life family, from how they make curricula decisions to whether their children take tests.

After spending their first twelve years searching for a homeschool method that met their Scriptural and educational criteria, they finally began using Christian textbooks and have never wanted to change direction again. In this book, Steve and Teri share the benefits their family has gained from using textbooks, and they refute the reasons many will say homeschoolers should not use textbooks.

There is a chapter written by four of the adult Maxwell children sharing some of their homeschool thoughts, particularly with regard to using Christian textbooks. The appendix of *Managers of Their Schools* includes ten of the Maxwell's school schedules, several assignment sheets, a listing of the school curricula and resources the Maxwells personally use, plus coupon codes for discounts on some of them.

Whether or not you use the same method to home educate as the Maxwells, you will find a wealth of tried-and-true, daily-life homeschool information. Make your homeschooling journey that much easier, more efficient, and more joyful by learning from a family who has already walked the path.

"I have learned so much from the book. The time I will save in planning for this school year is astronomical!" A mom

"The book was excellent! It was like somebody was taking your hand and gently leading you through the homeschool journey." A mom

"For the struggling homeschool family, it would be particularly helpful, but it would also give tips and scriptural support to the satisfied homeschool family as well." A mom

"Now we are getting more than our planned amount of school done on most days, and finishing early. This is an answer to my prayer that the Lord would streamline our schooling to provide more time for ministry and family." A mom

"This book fills a niche unspoken of by others in this field. And, oh, how exhilarating that is to my planning for next year. This book gave me the freedom to continue our journey without doubt, the encouragement to make the needed changes, and the insight to see how another family found solid answers and adjusted curricula to fit needs." A mom

"I have all three of the 'Managers' books (as well as some of your other books) and each one has been such a help to me. I return to them again and again for tips/ideas. The MOTS book is helping to revolutionize my homeschool. I felt as though a loving, successful, older homeschool mom, who had learned a great deal from her struggles (many of which are similar to my own), was speaking directly to me." A mom

"The book was well-written and thought provoking, with good use of examples and real-life testimonies to make it come alive and see how it could work for me." A mom

To order or for information visit: www.Titus2.com.
Or call: (913) 772-0392.

Homeschooling with a Meek and Quiet Spirit
by Teri Maxwell

The desire of a homeschooling mother's heart is to have a meek and quiet spirit instead of discouragement, fear, and anger.

Because Teri Maxwell, a mother of eight, has walked the homeschooling path since 1985, she knows first-hand the struggle for a meek and quiet spirit. The memories from her early homeschooling years of often being worried and angry rather than having a meek and quiet spirit are not what she would like them to be.

Will your journey toward a meek and quiet spirit be completed upon finding the perfect spelling curriculum or deciding which chores your child should be doing? Perhaps the answer lies on a different path.

In these pages, Teri offers practical insights into gaining a meek and quiet spirit that any mom can apply to her individual circumstances. She transparently shares the struggles God has brought her through and what He has shown her during these many homeschooling years.

As you read *Homeschooling with a Meek and Quiet Spirit,* you will discover the heart issues that will gently lead you to a meek and quiet spirit. Come along and join Teri as you seek the Lord to homeschool with a meek and quiet spirit!

A study guide is also available.

"This is one of the best, most helpful, encouraging, and empathetic books I've read during my 5 years of homeschooling." A mom

"I wish all moms, regardless of their school choice, could read Homeschooling with a Meek and Quiet Spirit." *Kathy*

"It is not just for homeschooling moms, but any mom who wants to be the best mom she can be. It was challenging, enlightening, and encouraging." A mom

**To order or for information visit: www.Titus2.com.
Or call: (913) 772-0392.**

Feed My Sheep
A Practical Guide to Daily Family Bible Time
by Steve Maxwell

Tried them and failed? Never tried because you knew it would be too big of a battle? No time for them even if you wanted to? Do any of these questions describe your experience with family Bible time? This two CD set is highly motivational and practical.

In the first CD, Steve Maxwell gives practical advice for achieving success with family Bible time. He reveals the secret that he guarantees will work

The second CD will help you gain ideas on how simple it is to implement a family Bible time as you join the Maxwell family for two of theirs. You'll feel like you're right at home with Steve as you listen to him lead his family in their time in the Word. You will see how easy it is to lead your family in the most important time of the day.

Join Steve, father of eight, as he shares about the Maxwells' favorite part of their day. We pray you'll come away with an excitement for the daily feeding of your family from God's Word!

To order or for information visit: www.Titus2.com.
Or call: (913) 772-0392.

Just Around the Corner
Encouragement and Challenge
for Christian Dads and Moms, Volumes 1 and 2

(Volume 3 Coming Soon!)
By Steven and Teri Maxwell

Just Around the Corner (Volumes 1 and 2) is a compilation of Steve and Teri Maxwell's monthly Dad's and Mom's Corners. These articles are written to help and challenge Christian parents, many of whom may not have grown up with godly role models.

Are you content with the way things are in your family? Do you feel like you are running on a treadmill? Do you want to have sweet relationships with your children as they are growing up and not experience the heartache of rebellion and immorality? Are you looking for practical guidance to a deeper family walk with Jesus Christ? These are a few of the topics addressed in these indexed books.

Steve's writing will challenge a dad in his role as the spiritual head of the family. Teri's writing addresses many aspects of daily life that often frustrate or discourage a mom. Authored by the parents of eight children, the two volumes provide encouragement that dads and moms are seeking for their personal walks with the Lord Jesus, their roles as husbands and wives, and the raising of their children. Through *Just Around the Corner*, the Maxwells want to show you ways—some of which you may never have imagined—that God can set your family on a spiritual journey.

"The Maxwells are so encouraging and down to earth. I had been feeling down about some negative behavior in my children, things in my marriage, homeschooling, and the list goes on. This book has helped me to regain my focus and carry on to what God has called me to do." Michelle

To order or for information visit: www.Titus2.com.
Or call: (913) 772-0392.

The Moody Family Series
Book #1: *Summer with the Moodys*
Book #2: *Autumn with the Moodys*
Book #3: *Winter with the Moodys*
Book #4: *Spring with the Moodys*
Book #5: *Summer Days with the Moodys*

By Sarah Maxwell

Often parents are concerned about negative examples and role models in books their children are reading. One goal in writing the Moody Series was to eliminate those kinds of examples replacing them with positive, godly ones.

In the books, you'll find the Moodys helping a widowed neighbor, starting small businesses for the children, enjoying a family fun night, training their new puppy, homeschooling, Mom experiencing morning sickness, and much more! Woven throughout the books is the Moodys' love for the Lord and their enjoyment of time together. Children (parents too!) will enjoy the Moody family—they'll come away challenged and encouraged.

"My six-year-old son asked Jesus into his heart while we were reading Autumn with the Moodys. *These books are wonderful, heart-warming Christian reading. The Moodys will always have a special place in our hearts!"* A mom

"At last, a Christian book series that is engaging and encourages my children to love Jesus more and bless their family and friends." A mom

To order or for information visit: www.Titus2.com.
Or call: (913) 772-0392.

Manager of His Home
Learning to Lead & Love Your Wife
By Steve Maxwell

Do you desire to know what practical, spiritual headship actually means, and does your wife long for this? How do you lead and still allow her to manage the home?

In this audio session you will be given real-life, biblical suggestions for how you can support and facilitate your wife in her role as a homeschooling mom.

"I would recommend this message to others because it provided plenty of practical, daily examples of how to lead the family." A dad

Sports—Friend or Foe?
By Steve Maxwell

Homeschooling families are heavily involved in sports. What are the parents' goals in having their children participate in organized sports? Are these goals being met? Are the children better or worse by being one of the team? Steve shares the Maxwells' experience on sports as well as incorporating data from a large on-line survey that he conducted regarding Christian families and sports.

Anger—Relationship Poison
By Steve & Teri Maxwell

Homeschooling families have a heart's desire to raise godly children. However, it seems that anger is found in many homeschooling parents, and it can undermine all the hours invested in positive teaching. It can destroy our most precious relationships. Have you noticed how certain levels of anger are accepted and justified? Do you have difficulty controlling your anger? Is a harsh tone in your voice anger? Steve and Teri will encourage you on this universally needed topic as they share from God's Word and personal testimonies.

Encouragement for the Homeschool Family
By the Maxwells

Encouragement for the Homeschool Family is an eight-session audio seminar which will encourage, exhort, and equip homeschooling families. Included in the album: *Building a Vision, Managers of Their Homes, Manager of His Home, Loving Your Husband, Sports–Friend or Foe, Anger–Relationship Poison, Experiencing the Joy of Young Womanhood,* and *Success or Failure–Where Are You Headed?* (for young men).

Building a Vision
By Steve & Teri Maxwell

Whether new or experienced homeschoolers, this motivational and practical session helps a family develop a godly vision for raising their children and then live according to that vision.

Together, Steve and Teri will give you concrete examples from homeschooling struggles they have experienced and how they made it through. With five adult children whom they homeschooled and three more children who are currently being homeschooled, they have the experience to know how to keep on while still being in the trenches of day to day homeschooling.

To order or for information visit: www.Titus2.com.
Or call: (913) 772-0392.

Loving Your Husband
By Teri Maxwell

This is an incredible session every woman should listen to. It is easy for a mom to become consumed with children and day-to-day life. This leaves the opportunity for creating a huge gap in her relationship with the key person in her life—her husband. Don't damage or lose that special relationship with your husband but rather develop and strengthen it.

Success or Failure– Where Are You Headed?
By Christopher Maxwell

Homeschooled young men have incredible potential for success in their lives—both spiritually and vocationally. There are tragic pitfalls that might appear innocuous on the surface to be avoided. In addition there are basic elements crucial for success in the spiritual world and in the business world. This session explores how the different aspects of a young man's life will affect his future.

Experiencing the Joy of Young Womanhood
By Sarah Maxwell

Sarah explores aspects of a young woman's life that lead to true joy. It all starts with the foundation—your relationship with Jesus Christ. She delves into hindrances to joy as well as practical aspects of it. Plenty of personal testimonies from Sarah's life are sprinkled into the session.

To order or for information visit: www.Titus2.com.
Or call: (913) 772-0392.

How to Start and Run Your Own Home Business
(for young people)
By Christopher & Sarah Maxwell

During your teen years, homeschool students have incredible opportunities to start, run, and build successful businesses. You will not only be earning income but also learning invaluable life skills. In this practical workshop, given by a brother and sister team, Christopher and Sarah Maxwell share how you can start your own business. You'll come away with specific ideas—and hopefully a big dose of motivation—to start your own business! Don't waste your teen years—do something beneficial!

Family Evangelism—Effectively Sharing Christ & Loving It
By Christopher Maxwell

While many believers might have a deep desire to see others saved, they aren't actively sharing their faith. From overcoming fear, to studying how Jesus witnessed to the lost, to the missing ingredient in modern evangelism, this session is designed to equip, motivate, and encourage you! You'll hear real life examples that resulted from everyday opportunities—opportunities that you can also experience.

To order or for information visit: www.Titus2.com.
Or call: (913) 772-0392.

Notes

Notes

Notes